ICE ON THE WING
Essays on Life and Other Difficult Situations

Ice On The Wing

Essays on Life and Other Difficult Situations

By

Shalynn Ford Womack

Nashville

These articles originally appeared in numerous publications, including: *The Huntsville (AL) Times*; *The Tennessean*; *The Tennessee Register*; *The (Moline, IL) Dispatch*; *Quad-City Times*; *The (Murfreesboro, TN) Daily News Journal*; *The National Catholic Reporter*; *Nashville Parent*; and *The Tullahoma (TN) News*. The publication date appears at the end of each article. This volume also contains some previously unpublished material.

Published by Spearhead Press
Nashville, Tennessee

Spearhead Press Logo Design by Nova Ford

For Nova, my true north and best source in matters great and small.

&

For Steve, who believes in me even when I don't believe in me.

Thank you both for using your considerable artistic, editorial, and technical talents to melt the ice. I am grateful.

In Memory
Of
Sister Germaine Cupp, O.S.B.

The world breaks everyone
and afterward many are strong
at the broken places. But those that will
not break, it kills. It kills the very good
and the very gentle and the very brave
impartially. If you are none of these
you can be sure it will kill you too,
but there will be no special hurry.
—Ernest Hemingway
A Farewell to Arms

TABLE OF CONTENTS

INTRODUCTION

*I**ce On The Wing** is, in many ways, almost a literary version of an archeological dig. The articles and essays presented in this anthology are remnants of an industry that no longer exists. These are relics and memories of a by-gone era, of a time (sometimes) fondly remembered and long past. The pieces in this book were written in the days before anyone ever heard the term *blogger*, before the emergence of social media, before writers put their work before the public by *tweeting* it. The columns, articles and essays contained in this anthology were printed on what was once called *hard copy*. These words are from a time when people read news by holding it in their hands, accompanied by the rustle of cheap newsprint as they flapped the pages, struggling to turn them without knocking over a coffee cup. When readers put these pages down, they saw the smudges of ink on their fingertips, felt the texture of the paper, and inhaled the dry, crisp aroma of a *newspaper*.

This wasn't digital journalism; it was *visceral*.

And Shalynn Ford Womack isn't a *content provider*, she's a *writer*.

For just over a dozen years, Shalynn Ford Womack made her living in an occupation that simply doesn't exist anymore—the regional freelance newspaper columnist. Starting in the spring of 1995, with a piece she sold to the Moline, Illinois *Dispatch*, Shalynn Ford Womack (writing most of the time as Shalynn Ford) began cultivating both editors and readers, growing her readership and her newspaper base until her columns were both popular and in great demand.

Now keep in mind, she was never actually employed by any of the newspapers she wrote for. As these columns will reveal, Shalynn Ford Womack has never been one to be tied down to a time clock, a single office or routine, or to lock herself into a career of taking assignments. As you'll see, her interests were too wide-ranging, and both her mind and nature were too restless to ever settle down into one outlet, one reader base, one community.

In her soul as well as her work, Shalynn Ford Womack is a *free-lancer*. And what are those interests? Put plainly and simply, Shalynn Ford Womack wrote about the world around her, the things that got under her skin, that fascinated her and troubled her. A divorced, single mother, she chose to homeschool her daughter, Nova. She wrote so many columns about Nova that her daughter practically grew up in the public eye. The journey, the adventure, and the struggles of homeschooling a child from kindergarten through twelfth grade are documented in these pages in a way that will make you laugh, make your heart hurt, make tears come to your eyes.

Shalynn's mother, Roseann, was a frequent topic as well. Roseann Gillespie contracted polio in the 1950s as a young woman in her early thirties, four years before Shalynn was born. And it's a testament to how strong this woman was that she not only managed to survive polio during a time when few did, but that she also gave birth to Shalynn after her illness and raised her alone. She lived to be ninety years old. Roseann and Shalynn had a relationship that was multi-layered and complicated—at times, tortured—and one that Shalynn bravely bared to her readers. She wrote about this life-long relationship with honesty and raw, sometimes agonizing, vulnerability.

Then there was the arena of politics. Shalynn Ford Womack has always described herself as a deeply committed, progressive Irish-Catholic Democrat, dedicated to social justice and service to the poor and disenfranchised. Oftentimes, her politically charged columns got her in trouble with orthodox Catholic readers and even the Church itself. As you'll see in these pages, that seldom—no, make that *never*—stopped her.

When she saw political injustice, intolerance or prejudice in society, or basic human unfairness, she turned her typewriter keys on it like a Tommy Gun. Sex discrimination, racial prejudice, poverty, right-wing politicians, bureaucracies—nothing was spared.

Curiously enough, she got away with it, especially given the roster of newspapers who carried her work. Shalynn Ford Womack wasn't published by the Eastern, elitist, liberal press, but rather by regional newspapers like *The Huntsville Times*; *The* (Moline, Illinois) *Dispatch*; *The Quad-City Times*; *The Tullahoma News*; and *The Tennessean*.

Her work appeared regularly in *The Tennessee Register*, the official publication of the Catholic Diocese of Nashville (until she finally really did tick off the Bishop, who also happened to be the paper's publisher). Regional magazines like *Nashville Parent* picked up her work as well. She didn't get rich, nor did she ever hit the big time, although the *New York Times* picked up four of her columns for syndication.

She wrote about life in general, the struggle to find satisfying relationships, the heartbreak and loss of divorce, the challenges of economic survival. Illness and loss, the death of loved ones and of dreams—all were grist for her mill. Born in a blue-collar, working class neighborhood in Moline, Illinois, she eventually earned three college degrees. She held several university-level teaching positions, as well as a host of other jobs, few of which gave her the satisfaction that being a freelance newspaper columnist did.

Ultimately, it all came to an end as the newspaper business went into decline. One editor explained to her that Hurricane Katrina in 2005 was a major turning point. In the wake of that disaster, fuel prices shot up and it became a lot more expensive to deliver home newspapers. Circulation numbers and advertising income was plunging thanks to the World Wide Web. Costs were going up across the board. A crisis was in the making.

Cuts had to be made, and the first ones to go were the freelancers. By 2008, as the economy crashed into the Great Recession, it was all over.

As you're about to see, though, while it lasted Shalynn Ford Womack wrote these columns with passion, a fierce intelligence, and often with some anger at the injustice she observed in daily life. There was also a softer side to many of these pieces, often revealing a dry, almost sardonic wit. There was a voice at work in these columns; one that was, in turns, loving, angry, sad, funny, poignant, bittersweet, and longing. Sometimes within the same paragraph, and usually within the 750 word limit imposed by her editors…

So welcome to ***Ice On The Wing***. Prepare to be moved, entertained, angered, saddened, and touched, on lots of different levels.

PART ONE

ICE ON THE WING

Essays on Life and Other Difficult Situations

ICE ON THE WING

"Will it always be this way?" she asked glumly. "Are we forever doomed to recreate the role of abandoned child in our adult relationships?"

"No," he replied, "someday it will be different. All obstacles will be removed. We'll get a level playing field…we'll find partners that are on the same page instead of reading out of a different book. And then we'll get the life we hoped for instead of the life we swore to avoid."

"Really?" She was beginning to feel oddly hopeful.

There was a long silence…

"No," he said finally. "It will never be any different. Every relationship will be another trip through the hall of mirrors. Some relationships will appear more distorted, others, less so. But the point is, they will all be distorted. And in the end, all we'll have is a long history of distortion."

"And," she added wearily, "Ice on the wing."

* * *

On December 12, 1985, six minutes after takeoff, Arrow Air Flight MF 1285R crashed into the rugged landscape of Gander, Newfoundland. All 248 passengers and eight crew members were killed. The official cause of the crash was listed as ice accumulation on the wings.

Ice on the wing. It can bring down a huge passenger plane. It can bring down princesses and prime ministers. And it can bring down love and other lofty illusions. In short, ice on the wing is a force to be reckoned with. It is also, I believe, the best way to explain the unexplainable—those random errors and accidents that seem to define daily life.

Two years ago, a reporter from one of our local television stations interviewed family members of some of the soldiers who died on Flight MF1285R. It was part of a tenth anniversary special commemorating soldiers from the 101st Airborne at nearby Ft. Campbell who had died on the doomed flight.

A woman who had lost her daughter on the flight told how the pain had never gone away. It was always there. Like a constant companion. Some days it was worse, other days, a little less painful. But it was always with her. As if it had just happened yesterday.

How in the world does a person ever make peace with a paradox like ice on the wing? Ice on the wing is not some exotic, complex disease that baffles the most brilliant minds in medicine. It is not about heroic self-sacrifice on a distant battlefield. It is not even the result of some silly daredevil adventure gone awry. Ice on the wing is just frozen water on the wrong thing at the wrong time. So simple. Yet fatal. Ironic. Just like life.

Ice on the wing comes in many forms. And it eventually comes to every zip code. An air bag deploys and decapitates a child who begged to ride in the front seat "just this once." People starve to death while tons of food is stockpiled nearby. A woman comes down with a head cold during the sixth month of her pregnancy and the baby is later born with severe birth defects. A day later, a day earlier, a simple head cold wouldn't have made a difference. But that precise day, the fetus was vulnerable.

A missed opportunity. A wrong left turn. A minor mistake. A chance encounter. A single event. Ice on the wing can be very subtle. At least initially. But then, that left turns proves fatal. The minor mistake leads to catastrophic consequences. The chance encounter results in tragedy. Or a single event changes the course of history.

Sometimes ice on the wing can even appear benign. Inconsequential. Even preordained. It is none of these. Ice on the wing is just bad stuff that happens and makes no apparent sense. And it pretty much defines life and other difficult situations. However, there is some good news: ice eventually melts. In the meantime, beware of the wing…

—May, 1997

BEYOND THE PLASTIC PRISON

On June 13, 1990, I became an inmate of the plastic prison—one of 880,339 people in America to file for bankruptcy. Since then, I have patiently listened to unsolicited sermons on fiscal responsibility, weathered scathing criticism of my spending habits (yes, it's possible that lipstick I once charged on my Visa pushed me over the financial edge, but since I'm still using that same tube of lipstick five years later, could you cut me some slack?), and faced hostile creditors (when I was seven months into a difficult pregnancy and they suggested I do whatever it takes to get a job, I was, admittedly, intimidated. I was too scared to ask what they meant by "whatever it takes"). In retrospect, I think the line of good taste was crossed. In time, however, I did come to question my very right to exist in a materialistic society sans credit.

I also did a lot of soul searching while doing time in the plastic prison. How did this fiscal nightmare become my reality? Am I really the deadbeat society says I am? Or, have we just become a society of plastic people mistaking wealth for worth? Will I ever have any self-respect? Is there life beyond the plastic prison?

Unfortunately, for all my introspection, the bottom line was pretty simple: I was just an ordinary person trying to live an ordinary life in extraordinary economic times. Clearly, I failed.

Fortunately, in every failure are sown the seeds for success. The trick is in the sorting. Often, success and failure bear an uncanny resemblance to one another. For example, failure to have more credit cards than lifespan is not a sign of personal worthlessness. Yet, there is a scene in the movie *Pretty Woman* where Richard Gere tells Julia Roberts that sales clerks are never nice to people, they're only nice to credit cards, and you notice the audience nodding their collective heads in agreement. So, the sorting is tricky.

Advertisements for bankruptcy promise a fresh start and financial relief. Take it from me, you'll get neither. The brief rendezvous with relief that I got lasted only as long as it took creditors to begin objecting to the payment plan (which they have the right to do).

After the objections came the depositions ("nothing to worry about" squawked the head legal eagle) and summary judgment made in our absence. It was not in our favor.

As I signed the agreement to pay an extra $10,000 *not* included in our bankruptcy, I asked the paralegal how this fiasco happened. Her reply: you went into federal bankruptcy court to seek relief from creditors that included the federal government. Bad move. Persecution and prosecution can look a lot alike.

Next came the humility. Mine. Imagine having to justify your need for three haircuts a year ("is this expense really necessary?"). Same with groceries, diapers, laundry. Everything must be accounted for and approved by people I'd never met.

Suddenly, I was inmate #390-06033. Less of a person with less needs, less rights, less worth. Worse, I was a pregnant inmate. My unborn daughter became known on public record as "a willful act by the debtor to avoid repayment." My difficult pregnancy had been costly, but publicly labeling an unborn child in such a degrading way seemed particularly mean spirited. Did it make me more repentant for my crime of poverty? Did it speed up the repayment process? Hardly. Instead, it lent validity to the bad press attorneys receive. For the most part, the legal profession is comprised of a frightening bunch of megalomaniacs who prey on the misery of others for every billable hour possible.

My incarceration in the plastic prison has been a learning experience I won't soon forget. Now, I know who my real friends are. And aren't. I also realize I am not the sum total of my credit. I am much more. And I will never allow my identity and my credit limit to become inextricably bound again.

This morning, I was released from the plastic prison. Eight months ahead of schedule. Early parole through good behavior and frugal living. Inmate #390-06033 is finally free. Paid in full. Case closed.

—December 23, 1994 *The Tennessean*

IF I ONLY HAD A WIFE

Today has been a rare day for me. It has been a day free of inter-ruptions, requests for attention, fractured thoughts, incomplete sentences, and mind-numbingly repetitious tasks. In short, it's been a day off from my career as 'perfect' mom. Of course, parents never really get a day off once drafted into the baby stroller brigade, but now and then, someone (in this case, my daughter's father) comes along and offers the illusion of freedom by taking your offspring for a few hours, or even an entire day. Suddenly, I have the oppor-tunity to do something for just me. Who??? *Me?* Do I even exist independent of my role as 'mom'? Lately, I've been wondering. It's crossed my mind more than once that while laboring to birth my child, I may have pushed too hard and delivered a part of myself in the process.

When my daughter, Nova, was born, I never had a single doubt about spending all my time with her. She was the center of my uni-verse and I was blissfully happy. Life was simple and idyllic that first year.

When Nova was thirteen months old, I started teaching again. I taught one class, Child Psychology. Essentially, I was teaching what I was living. A colleague took care of Nova while I taught my class twice a week. No daycare for my child. I was determined to be the 'perfect' mom. I read the latest research on child development and wrote lectures while Nova took her naps. After she went to bed for the evening, I graded papers and exams. I doubt she even knew I worked. My daughter had June Cleaver and Hillary Clinton rolled into one 'perfect' mom. That was the second year.

The following year, my husband and I separated. I no longer had the luxury of a wife job, that is, the privilege of recreational em-ployment. Wife jobs, as I define them, are different from real jobs in that they generate discretionary income. Real jobs generate nec-essary income. Gone also was the luxury of time. My new compan-ions were anger, guilt, and fear. In time, I learned that the biggest problem with perfection, whether it's being the perfect wife, daughter, mother, or all three, while trying to live the perfect life, is that impossible standards must constantly compete with the relentless realities of life. Real life always wins.

I began to envy women like my friend, Jenny. Jenny is the consummate career woman whose children were destined for daycare in utero. For Jenny, and many other women, there is little or no dilemma about children and careers. They love their work and would not consider giving it up. They love their children, too, but they would never define themselves primarily as mothers. Maybe they did not push quite as hard, preserving their separateness in a way I seem incapable of. My child, myself. The line of demarcation only grew more blurred with the passage of time. I felt lost and confused in a world of shifting roles. That was the third year.

Last year, I went to work full-time. For all of one semester. Along with my teaching duties, I also participated in several conferences and even did some freelance writing. Amazingly enough, I also managed to preserve the illusion of 'perfect' mom by attending every preschool event, taking my daughter along to every conference (I'd pit her geography skills against anyone twice her age), memorizing the theme songs to both *Aladdin* & *The Lion King*, and baking a lot of cookies.

There was, admittedly, an incredible sense of accomplishment that went with keeping so many balls in the air. There was also incredible exhaustion. And, there was the nagging question of what was really being accomplished by such heroic efforts at professional and personal perfection. Finally, the exhaustion grew bigger than me. So, I swallowed my pride, and like others before me, put my professional dreams on the shelf, called my daughter's father, and asked about reconciliation. That was the fourth year.

Recently, I got a call from my boss. My current part-time teaching job was going full-time in the fall. And it included a promotion to Assistant Professor. I had a choice to make: full-time or no time. Peace of mind seems to elude me.

I began doing a lot of soul searching. Two-thirds of the faculty in higher education are male. Over 80% have a doctorate degree. I am a female with a Master's degree. Accepting this offer would be a professional coup. It would also mean an incredible investment of time and energy. And, as luck would have it, this was also the year I would begin homeschooling my daughter (perfect moms, perfect mentors—it must be a curse of some sort).

I consulted with my colleagues—mostly men—who were openly puzzled by my dilemma. I tried to explain the importance of a parental promise. That my time with my child is so limited. That in the blink of an eye, she'll be grown and gone. This precious time comes around only once. Teaching jobs, any job, for that matter will always be available in some form. They just didn't get it. Every one of my male friends had a wife who had generously shelved her own dreams to run a home and raise children. Those sacrifices had enabled my colleagues to make real choices. If I only had a wife, I lamented. But I didn't. Instead, I faced a choice that would force a sacrifice.

My child or my career. In theory, I can have both. In reality, having two full-time jobs means one gets relegated "second" job status. Nobody can be 100% in a 200% equation.

In retrospect, I'm sure I'd made my decision long before I consciously realized it. I declined the job offer. Bad timing, I explained. My boss' reply, "there will never be a good time for you," really hit home. He may be right.

While women represent the majority of the work*force*, the work*place* remains the province of men—and women like Jenny who refuse to yield to the feminine tradition of forced choice. For now, and maybe always, my choice is to take the professional path less traveled. However, Hillary Clinton has been a powerful role model. Someday, I will be back in the classroom and on the conference circuit. Meanwhile, move over, June Cleaver, I've got a killer cookie recipe that my daughter and her friends love. This is the fifth year.

—June 22, 1995 *Quad-City Times*

ROAD MAP TO REALITY

Recently, the movie *Hook* made its television debut. My daughter was elated at the prospect of seeing her favorite Peter Pan characters come to life. Her excitement, however, vanished quicker than pixie dust when she saw what had become of Peter Pan. "He's grown up," she observed dejectedly. "He promised he'd never grow up. *Ever.* This movie is ruined."

Yes, the cinematic version had indeed grown up. Boring. Predictable. Very Hollywood. I told my pint-sized vision of despair not to worry. Almost every female over twelve has experienced a very different scenario—harsh reality.

Dating, for example, has always been a dicey proposition. Most women have at least one war story about the date from hell. Some women eventually have enough material for a mini-series, unresolvable sequel, and lifelong commitment to therapy. A few women have even survived an encounter (not to be mistaken for a relationship) with a truly dysfunctional dating partner. Far from charmingly neurotic, this guy is the Ebola virus of the dating circuit—relatively rare, but always deadly.

Facing another Valentine's Day gouging out the bottoms of a two pound box of Godiva chocolates (I hate surprises) to pass the time prompts me to reflect on my own past 'encounters.' Thus, in the interest of public service and personal catharsis, I have compiled a list of psychological mile markers that will help women spot a deadly dating partner, *aka* the Peter Pan Quasi-Man (PPQ-M). If you recognize your (in)significant other, report to your nearest mental health center for an injection of self-esteem and a road map back to reality. It's the only known antidote for even a brief encounter with a toxic variation of the usually benign testosterone type genus:

1. He is rule-bound to the total exclusion of anything that smacks of spontaneity. He has boundary issues, e.g., he categorically forbids you to phone him at home on the pretense it violates his personal space. Translation: He's terrified his mother will answer the phone and find out her pot roast isn't all that's cooking.

2. He's a diagnosable control freak. Sometime during a series of midlife crises, the hormone Nositol reached a toxic level in his bloodstream, and while this condition is not usually fatal, it does result in extreme social impotence that looks at lot like protracted adolescence. Translation: He will never grow up and you will only grow old and bitter waiting for the impossible.

3. His erratic behavior and mercurial mood swings will leave *you* in a state of permanent mental meltdown. And then he'll leave you because, "you're crazy." Translation: Love and war are one and the same. Remember what happened to Captain Hook in the end?

4. He's smoother than a silkworm. Translation: A worm in a silk suit is still slimy.

5. He is the prince of plastic promises. He can't bend (refer back to numbers one and two), so ultimately, his promises are worthless. Translation: Plastic people break promises and hearts. If you're looking for plastic, get a credit card. At least the interest is real.

6. He is a connoisseur of small talk, has a lot of friendly ac-quaintances, and a full social calendar. Yet, something is obviously missing. Translation: that something is substance.

7. He is extraordinarily narcissistic. On the upside, he is always well-groomed. The downside is that everything, including your right to exist in his egocentric universe hinges on his precarious whim. Translation: It's all about *him*.

8. He pontificates about communication, respect, and honesty. Still he always fails the ultimate litmus test of sincerity: commit-ment. Utter the 'c' word and be prepared for a disappearing act that would rival Houdini's best performance. Translation: The rhetoric will never become reality.

9. He always returns to Never Never Land, so unless you're pre-pared to spend your life on Prozac while waiting for him to occa-sionally grace your life with his rakish presence, forget the boy toy and move on. Translation: None needed.

It is now known that the PPQ-M suffers from the rare chromo-somal abnormality, *non committere abilite*. There is no known cure. Anything that smacks of normalcy causes the PPQ-M to scatter like pixie dust in the wind. In fact, catching Tinker Bell's magic dust would be a far easier task. And much more realistic.

Chocolate, anyone?

—February 11, 1996 *The Tennessee Register*
—February 13, 1997 *The Dispatch*

FOR BETTER AND WORSE

I did not want to go there in the beginning. It was just another inconvenience. Another fly in the ointment. Another change. But, I didn't seem to have a choice. Our Meals-On-Wheels delivery route had been changed. Effective immediately. The new and un-improved in-the-middle-of-nowhere route. New faces, new places. The rural South. Might as well be the end of the earth, I grumbled.

Everett Parker, 74, lives on the edge. Of town and life. And had it not been for the route change, our paths would never have crossed. Fortunately, small inconveniences sometimes lead to important discoveries. Serendipity. And valuable life lessons.

Parker's house—all 500 square feet of it—sits way back, up the hill from the main highway to town. I missed it on the first pass. And the second. Frankly, I didn't even think "it" was a house. Too small. Too shabby. And too far off the beaten path.

An assortment of ancient vehicles take up one entire side of the front yard. Near the house, an herb garden, once tended by Parker's wife, Julia, struggles to survive amidst the thriving crabgrass. On the other side of the yard, numerous pine and maple trees provide ample shade. And, scattered throughout the abandoned yard, a few tiny daffodils bloom. Proof that beauty survives. Even here.

I walk up the dirt path and knock on the wooden screen door. A man's voice invites me to come in. I hesitate. Peering through the doorway, I can see nothing. Pitch black. And it's nearly noon. Finally, a small lizard scampering across the porch prompts me to step into the darkness.

He is legally blind. That's why the lights are off, he explains. It doesn't make any difference. He apologizes. A light snaps on. That's when I first see him. And then her.

He is sitting in a chair, legs propped up on a footstool. In a nearby recliner, she sits, staring off in the distance.

Advanced Alzheimer's, he tells me. At first, she sang old church hymns all night. Now, five years later, she is nearly catatonic. He will not put her in a nursing home, Parker tells me, because, 55 years ago, "I promised for better and worse and I always keep my promises." Besides, Parker continues, "when I got hurt 19 years ago, she took good care of me."

He tells me about the construction accident that left him permanently disabled. His legs, a mottled reddish-purple mess from the knees down, are infected with gout. Possibly gangrene. "They need to be amputated," Parker admits. But then he wouldn't be able to keep his promise.

I look over at what remains of his wife. Occasionally, she mumbles incoherently. Long periods of eerie silence follow. She weighs only 85 pounds, Parker comments ruefully. Her food must go through a blender. And sometimes, she won't eat at all. "She always wore a smile. And never, ever knew a stranger." His eyes mist. "It breaks my heart to see her like this."

During subsequent visits, he reminisces about his two grown children. His beloved son, a Vietnam veteran, suffered from depression, and tragically committed suicide nine years ago. His daughter, a nurse, lives in Arkansas. He speaks with love and pride, often pointing to dozens of family photos that adorn the living room walls. They are a source of comfort, he says. Soothing memories. The past preserved. Safe from the pain of the present.

It's ironic. I didn't want to go there in the beginning. Now, six months later, I can't stay away. I am drawn to this remarkable man who never complains. He is the same age my dad would be if he'd lived. And he sees incredibly well for someone who is blind. He sees the importance of loyalty. Honor. And keeping a promise. Maybe that's why I take him cupcakes and cornbread. I want him to know he matters. That he is not forgotten.

"She's not doin' so good," he reports during my most recent visit. No, she's not. Her frail body, rolled up in a fetal position, is barely visible beneath the mound of blankets covering her. She is silent, her mind somewhere else. Only a physical shell remains. And a promise from the heart of someone who loves her dearly.

For better and worse. For always. It is a valuable life lesson.

—April, 1996 *The Tennessee Register*

Author's Note: Julia Parker died one week later. Everett Parker, against the advice of his doctors, but comforted by memories of his beloved wife, remained in his home until his death one year later.

A FEW GOOD WOMEN

Memo to Mom: You were right. The prince is not coming. But there are a few good women out there. Happy Mother's Day.

Through the years, most of my friends have been men. Of course, most of my problems through the years have also been men. But that's another column. Today, I want to pay tribute to several remarkable women, near and far, who have shaped my life in some form or fashion. Each has left a vivid impression on a woman not easily impressed.

First, my mother, Roseann Gillespie. "Never forget those less fortunate," she always said. "Remember, they could be you." But for the grace of God...poor, elderly, homeless. Disenfranchised. I remember, Mom. Every time I pick up an ink pen, I remember. So, I use my pen to give voice to those who might otherwise go unheard. I may not be a perfect daughter, but at least I've never voted Republican. I'd never betray the woman who put her life on the line so I could have one, too.

Next, my daughter, Nova James. Through her, I have experienced something quite unfamiliar: hope. The aging Cinderella in me finds Nova's "I can do it all by myself" stance incredibly inspiring. Thanks for being such a great role model of empowerment. A babe with a brain. Someday, you'll make a real difference. And I'll be First Mother.

I probably wouldn't be a mother at all if it weren't for a wonderful doctor named Sherrie Richards. Six years ago, I spent Mother's Day exactly the same way I had spent the previous 72 days: throwing up. All day. Every day. Welcome to pregnancy. I can't do this. Just let me die. But Sherrie promised I could do it. And she delivered. No patronizing "It's all in your head, dear." Just plenty of empathy and support. A real breath of fresh feminist air. Bonus: While male colleagues are out golfing, Sherrie's keeping up with the latest research. That means I may get to keep some of those body parts I've grown accustomed to a little longer. It's nice to have a doctor on the *non*-cutting edge.

Looking good is next to feeling good. Okay, I'm vain. I admit it. Somewhere, there's a Wonderbra with my name on it. And one of those gruesome suck-it-up body shapers that boasts more wires than the average suspension bridge. Unlike the rest of me, my hair will never fall. For this small miracle, I have Tina Prow, hairstylist from heaven, to thank. When I first met Tina, she was 19. I was… older. But, three hours later, I looked considerably younger. In nine years, Tina has cut, crimped, curled, teased, texturized, bleached, bobbed, shagged, streaked, and straightened my hair in more colors and coifs than Hillary ever dreamed of. For years, I sported major mall hair. Then, at 35, I had 13 ½ inches cut off. So that's what a grown-up looks like. No, thanks. No more utilitarian 'dos for me. Looking like an adult is highly overrated. And really frightening. The only thing scarier would be facing my true hair color. What is my true hair color? Get a grip. I'd sooner reveal my mother's real age.

Next to God, industrial strength undergarments, and a talented hairstylist, everything else pales. Except my Tuesday night women's group. Last November, two women from St. Luke's Church had one radical idea: offer women an emotional sanctuary—a place where they feel safe, loved, accepted—and they can survive just about anything. No questions asked. Just show up. Fully present and engaged. And we do. Every Tuesday night, a small group of women gather in the church building to discuss everything from dill pickles to divorce. It's not therapy lite. It's not a "let's do lunch" thing. It's about love. Tolerance. Solidarity. Things women often deny other women. Thanks to Jo Haynes and Wanda Corbitt, nine women who might never have met, are now the best of friends. We represent a variety of values, backgrounds, and circumstances. Still, we view the world through the common lens of our gender. We have known good times and bad. And now we know each other. None of us will ever be alone again.

Last, but certainly not least, Hillary Rodham Clinton. Four years ago, my biggest accomplishment was a shiny floor. My Reagan Era-induced coma had taken its toll. Then came a blonde dynamo with the moxie to turn a nation on its ear. Thanks for the wake-up call. You've been a powerful role model. If you hadn't shown up just when you did, I would have drowned in my own cookie dough.

Strength of character. Personal integrity. The ability to love and nurture. Women of worth. Each of these is you. Happy Mother's Day.

—May 6, 1996 *The Tennessee Register*

THE ETHICS OF EDEN

The floor is very clean. I notice this because it is unusual for a public health clinic to have spotless floors. No kids playing, spilled drinks, or patients throwing up, either. Just a spotless floor and mind-numbing silence.

There are four men, one girl about sixteen or seventeen, her mother, and me sitting quietly in the waiting area. The girl is called first. She gets up and goes to the front desk. A moment later, her mother is at her side. In a loud whisper, the girl says, "It's negative. Let's go."

Her mother confirms this with the receptionist. She appears relieved. Until she realizes something. And then, another loud whisper. This time, it's the mother. "Did you tell them about last month?"

"Don't matter," replies the girl, nonchalantly. "Test is negative today."

Her mother isn't convinced.

The receptionist patiently explains that today's test results are good only for today. If there's another "exposure" you have to be retested. And no, last month's "exposure" will not show up on today's test. Four to six months must pass between the time of "exposure" and the test.

The girl promises to schedule another test in three months. She does not appear concerned. Today, the test results are negative. And today is all that matters.

After a short while, my name is called. The counselor, Brad, wants to know what brings me to the clinic today.

"I need to be tested for..." I stop. If I say it, I might have it. I don't dare say it. But I have to say it. Get a grip, I tell myself. "HIV." Finally. Each letter feels weighted in lead.

"Do you have reason to believe that you've been exposed to the HIV virus?" Brad is very casual. Like we're discussing the weather. Nice day to die, don't you think? A little humid, but the breeze feels nice.

"No." I just thought it would be kind of interesting to spend the afternoon at a public health clinic and see how the other half lives. Bored writer in search of a story. By the way, is it really true that the number of women with AIDS is doubling every 1-2 years?

"Yes."

Is it really the leading cause of death for women ages 25-44 in almost a dozen cities in the U.S.?

"It is."

And do heterosexual, married women really represent a new high risk group?

Brad's not sure about that one.

I explain how several recent studies found that married women are at high risk because they're counting on two things: fidelity and truth. And they're getting neither. Now we're getting closer to my agenda...

I digress. I do that when I'm anxious. I revise my earlier 'no' to "maybe." Now I'm going to explain. It's third grade and Sister has caught me being naughty. Confession is imminent.

I tell Brad about the letter I received one year ago today. The one that began, "This is going to be a very difficult letter for me to write..."

Good news did not follow. A former boyfriend had felt compelled to confess his infidelity ex post facto. There probably wasn't anything to worry about, he promised. He just thought I should know there had been others. In case.

In case of *what?*

Lest Brad think I am one of *those* people (read: loose), I clarify that Mr. Duplicity was someone I had known for twelve years. A college professor. A trusted colleague. Hardly the face of HIV.

Brad smiles patiently. I won't be the last idiot he sees today.

After the nurse takes a blood sample, I leave. The back way. Quietly. Anonymously. From now on, I will be known only as 0018299194. And in two weeks, the results will be back.

Two weeks feel like two years. What if it's positive? How will I tell my daughter? *What* will I tell her? That I made a stupid mistake a long time ago and it's come back to haunt me? That trust is toxic? That love is fatal? This is where the rubber meets the road. And speaking of…do I work in a lecture on the 'c' word? Condoms. That bane of the Catholic Church.

Sorry, Rome. With all due respect to the pope, the Ethics of Eden do not apply here. This is about real life. And death. This isn't about those trips to the clinic we made in our twenties. Pregnancy is not fatal. Of course, we used to think so. Every pregnancy test was supposed to be the last. Until the next Mr. Prince came along and promised the moon. The we'd slip on the same banana peel. Brain-Stuck-In-Skirt-Zipper-Syndrome. Catholic girls. Counting on miracles instead of ourselves.

Then we got older and bolder. We learned to assert ourselves. Unlike our mothers, we did not have to conceive and commit for a lifetime. We were no longer bound by the Ethics of Eden. But then came HIV. A major fly in the ointment.

Finally, two weeks are up.

The floor is just as clean today. A different counselor, Dederick, calls me into his office. "Negative," he announces, handing me a copy of the results. "Did you have concerns?"

"No. Well, maybe." Here we go again. "Yes." I go through the entire story of betrayal again. "So what's the solution?" If trust is the basis for a relationship, but you can't trust anyone (as both research and personal experience have proven), where does that leave romance? Still looking for the fairy tale. No wonder I'm so disillusioned.

"Spiritual fulfillment and non-sexual forms of intimacy," Dederick offers. "Too many people seek intimacy through a physical connection when what they really need is a spiritual connection. That's the only permanent connection we'll ever have, anyway. And the only one we can trust completely."

Dederick hands me a sheet of paper titled, *How Well Do You Know The 63 People You Slept With Last Night?* A diagram resembling a family tree illustrates how just one unfaithful partner can increase exponentially the risk of exposure to HIV. Very cozy. And very deadly. It will stay in my purse as a reminder. *Caveat emptor.*

"I hope I never see you again," Dederick smiles as I leave.

He won't. At least not through my own doing. I realize now that HIV really means Honesty Is Vital. I will never accept less. My life depends on it.   —September 8, 1996 *The Tennessean*

THE *CHEERS* CHURCH

Today is my birthday. Thirty-eight. Pass the Prozac. Tea and sympathy. Chocolate would also be appreciated, and a really good wrinkle cream.

It's been a really bizarre year. Both death and divorce have visited my zip code. In the blink of an eye, TWA Flight 800 and all the dreams it carried exploded in a mysterious fireball. Same with my marriage. No survivors. The shadow of death reached 13,000 feet as easily as it did a small town in Tennessee. A grim reminder that whether it's a bomb in Atlanta or over the Atlantic, there is no escape. Nobody's ticket is stamped exempt. Loss, loneliness, and death will come. Even to the best neighborhoods.

Across the sea, my royal soulmate lost both her crown and position as career wife. I can relate. My own personal version of Bill Clinton recently resurfaced in my life just long enough to break my heart again. I was almost Hillary. So much for fairy tales. They always go awry. For me, it seems to happen every election cycle. I know. Poetic justice.

On the other hand, supermodel Christie Brinkley did find another man to marry her—number four—upsetting the law of supply and demand for the rest of us. However, Don Johnson is single again, and back on the small screen in a role he seems eminently suited for—cop with a complicated personal life, an Armani vision of despair. At least Friday nights are once again bearable. And then there's Madonna, joining the great sorority of motherhood. Is the world ready for Madonna Reed?

Seems 1996 was destined to be just one Kodak moment after another. Picture perfect pain, pleasure, and paradoxes.

I need a sanctuary from all the sadness, the suffering, the sensation seeking. I need some succor, spiritual soothing, renewal. Most of all, I need relating, not recrimination. Even one hour will do, and then I can be camera-ready once again.

Baby boomers. Such an unhappy lot. We are compulsively driven to overachieve in a relentless, unforgiving, anxiety-ridden world of our own design. Imprisoned by our own technology, we are also an isolated bunch. We define ourselves in terms of despair and disillusionment, and then we watch, helplessly, as our relationships collapse under the weight of our sustained cynicism. Can't get no satisfaction, as the song goes. Yet, we continue to search for the illusion of intimacy, a sense of connectedness, someone to affirm our specialness, someone to tell us we matter.

Anybody...anything...will do: the one night stand, the bottle, the white powder, obsessing over the bottom line, power shopping, chocolate, even the church.

We are, it seems, from cradle to grave, attachment addicts. Anxiety reduction in a bottle, bag, or building. Just stop the pain.

Unfortunately, we're more choosy about selecting sunscreen than venues for our salvation. Luckily, there is a 300-watt beacon of light in this sea of anomie, right here in Hollywood South: St. Edward Church, a refuge for thinking Catholics who have evolved beyond basic dogma, a place where debate and dialogue are encouraged, where innovation coexists with tradition. The *Cheers* church where "everybody knows your name and they're always glad you came," especially Father Joseph Breen, pastor and human-being extraordinaire.

Week after week, year after year, Father Breen has shared his vision of inclusion with the congregation of St. Edward, preaching and practicing forgiveness, acceptance, tolerance, humanitarianism, a commitment to social justice, and real world ethics grounded in the compassion of Christ's teaching, all in the context of our relationship with God. Emphasis on relationship, not rules.

Rules provide only the most basic structure and parameters. Form without substance. Only a personal relationship with God offers real substance—depth, peace, a quiet heart. All the things we're searching for.

So refreshing to know a pastor who actually *gets it*.

Without the relationship, the rules are meaningless. Psychologist Carl Jung studied man's eternal quest for absolution and concluded, "Innocence cannot be restored, but forgiveness can be given." Only then can we, as individuals, experience the restorative power of redemption. Only then can we, as a church, call ourselves healthy. And isn't the ability to empathize with others the hallmark feature of a civilized society?

Fortunately, Father Breen and others like him are committed to providing an accepting milieu of forgiveness that encourages the disquieted to revisit their faith. A place where you're welcomed even if your resume of personal failures dwarfs your list of successes. Or your past is less than pristine. You—not your mistakes—matter.

Leaving St. Edward, I always feel spiritually refreshed, revived, renewed, redeemed. My raw psyche has been soothed. I can face tomorrow and all its uncertainty. One hour has made an incredible difference.

My innocence may never be restored, but forgiveness appears eminently attainable. Finally, my search is over.

Keep that light shining, Father Breen. Others are searching. More will be coming.

—October 7, 1996 The Tennessee Register

Author's Note: On December 20, 2011, the Reverend Joseph Patrick Breen celebrated the 50th anniversary of his ordination. A month earlier, over 700 people, including the Mayor of Nashville and the former Governor of Tennessee, attended his Golden Jubilee Celebration and paid tribute to his lifelong commitment to social justice. "Joe Pat" remains the beloved Pastor of St. Edward Church, where his legacy of inclusion continues.

Pain: The Gatekeeper to Paradise

We met in the first grade at St. Mary's. He sat three rows over from me. But Kevin lived a world away in the land of rowdiness, spirited antics, and sassiness that naughty little boys call home.

I didn't have much to do with him. Boys. The bane of six-year-old girls. Besides, I was the quintessential good girl. I wore a rosary around my neck, chose noon Mass over recess, and planned to be a nun when I grew up. I had no time for the Kevins of this world. By the fourth grade, he was gone. Expelled.

One day, eight years later, walking past the corner gas station, I heard someone whistle at me. A common occurrence when you're seventeen. I would have kept walking, but when I heard my name follow the adolescent male mating call, I stopped to see who was behind the voice. Kevin. Just my luck. The naughtiest boy from St. Mary's was flirting with me. Where had he been for the last eight years? In trouble, no doubt.

I was, admittedly, curious. The sinners always seem to lead more interesting lives than the saints. So I stayed and visited. I also went back the next day. And the next. Almost the entire summer. He turned out to be an incredibly engaging conversationalist.

One day, I stopped by the gas station and he wasn't there. He'd quit the day before. I couldn't believe it. And then it hit me for the first time. I had a major crush on the altar boy gone awry. But it was not to be.

Twenty years would pass before I'd see Kevin again. Still, I kept up with him through the newspaper. He was hard to miss. A one man crime wave in a small town is usually a headline grabber. And then there was the *big* story. Past sexual abuse, two respected adults, their admission of guilt, and the scandal that followed. Suddenly, everything fell into place. While most of us had relatively unremarkable childhoods, Kevin had lived a nightmare. Alone. Afraid. And abused by those we've been taught to trust. They say hell is for children. It certainly was for Kevin. I felt helpless. Angry. Sad. And, I mourned for the little boy who had his innocence taken from him all those years ago.

Six months ago, I attended my class reunion. Coincidentally, the local public high school was holding their class reunion in the same convention center. Tired of all my neurotic classmates and their overachievements, I wandered over to the Moline High School reunion. Slumming it. Looking for my grade school pals that had chosen public high school.

That's when I first saw—heard—them from across the room. The familiar sound of their laughter. Their ease. And good-natured humor. Just as I remembered it. Outward appearances had changed, but the intense camaraderie remained. The boys of St. Mary's had grown into men of worth. Including Kevin. Against all odds.

I asked Kevin how in the world he ever managed to turn such a troubled life around. I want to know his secret. Maybe it will work for me.

His answer: God. Pure and simple. "And learning that I have real choices."

He recounted the time when he'd hit rock bottom and decided to end his life. At the last possible moment, he'd felt God's presence so strongly that it stopped him from pulling the trigger. The experience left him deeply shaken, but determined to choose life—in spite of its certain cruelty. And he did.

First, an active commitment to repair his relationship with God. Next, the long road to recovery from alcohol and substance abuse. Then, learning to parent his two children. And finally, revealing the horrible truth he'd hidden for so long. The years of secret abuse. Betrayal. And broken promises.

It is said that pain is the gatekeeper to paradise. If anyone knows this, it's Kevin. His life has been largely shaped by pain. Lost innocence. And tragedy. Still, he has managed to say yes to life and to God's plan. It's simple, he tells me, but never easy. "You have two choices in life—pray or worry. You can't choose both. Just like you can't turn both left and right. If you pray, don't worry. In God's hands, everything works out. If you worry, don't bother to pray. There's no trust. And without trust, there's no relationship with God." Simple, but not easy.

Today, Kevin runs a successful business, sponsors newly recovering alcoholics, and is raising his two children by himself. He is a success story. An inspiration to those of us still struggling with the pain of a past imperfect. Proof that second chances are possible. And he's my friend. For that, I am truly blessed.

—December 16, 1996 *The Tennessee Register*

THE RAGE STAGE

Each year, approximately 2-3 million women are beaten by their partners. Domestic violence is the reason for more visits to the emergency room than all rapes, auto accidents, and muggings combined.

I have heard many stories of abuse over the years. Being a woman, former therapist, and writer, I get around. The following story is actually about many women…

It's nearly midnight. All's quiet in the lobby of the emergency room. Only three people still wait to see a doctor.

A shift worker naps quietly while he waits to have his blood pressure taken. A young girl waits on a pregnancy test. And a quiet woman sits across the room. She wears a brace on her right arm. From the last time she was here.

Waiting for her name to be called, she considers whether she has time to use the restroom. Probably not. Besides, that would mean having to get up. And then, being alone. She also realizes if she waits much longer, she may start thinking. Which could lead to more thinking. More pain. Rage. Grief. Hopelessness. More of everything she's had too much of lately.

The nurse finally calls her name. A brief reprieve. She slowly stands and tries to walk. A few feet seems like a mile down the road. Now she'll have to sit again. Reverse procedure. Slowly. Gently. Minimal movement. She is finally seated.

The nurse takes her blood pressure and temperature. And then comes the question she's been dreading. *How did this happen?*

How *did* this happen? The rage stage. The mistake that won't die. The rules. The history. The futility. Did she learn nothing from growing up in the house of horrors? Was her Catholic education a total waste? And what about that Catholic milieu that non-Catholics will never comprehend? The martyr mom milieu. The self-sacrifice. The unbendable, unforgiving rules.

How did this happen? Shame. Shame. Shame. The chorus of disappointment from the sisters at St. Anne's rings through her head. Didn't they teach her better?

Her head is an unquiet place of turmoil. The self-interrogation begins: *I screwed up, Sister. Bless me, Father, for I have sinned. Years ago, I made a mistake. I did the unforgivable. I got married. Worse, I married the wrong person. Yes, I know my penance. Life. No chance of parole. So, lately, I've been praying for a short life. My prayers were almost answered tonight.*

The problem, Father, is my daughter. She's the same age I was when my parents divorced. Once upon a time, I was her. Someday, she'll be me. Correction. She is me. Ironic, isn't it? Except her parents will not be divorced. Divorce is failure and failure is not an option. Until death do us part. You taught me well, Father.

In the meantime, I could use some help with answering my daughter's difficult questions and painful remarks. For example, when I commented recently about how popular she is with her friends (who are all boys), she said, "Well, they're okay for friends, but I will never marry any of them. Of course, I'm never going to marry anybody. Never." Adamant. I know that look. I own a mirror.

"How come?" Just curious. "Look at you, Mom. You're just a servant." There was a look of pity in her eyes. "Like Cinderella without a prince." True. But at least I'm Mrs. Servant. As opposed to Ms. Nobody. I'm married, therefore I am…somebody. One man away from invisibility. One man away from poverty.

Yes, Father, we've tried counseling. Many times. They said we had fundamental core differences that would prevent us from ever really connecting. I know. Just so much psycho babble. No excuses.

Yes, we've tried separation. The best few years of my recent life. Until I went back. Broken families. Broken bones. Broken dreams. Broken lives. Emphasis on broken. But still camera-ready at a moment's notice. The picture perfect family. Who would have ever thought?

I know I should have smiled a little brighter. Tried a little harder. Looked a little further. Somewhere in my house, there was more than a familiar stranger. I just couldn't find him.

"*How* did this happen?" the nurse repeats irritably.

She realizes she's been thinking again. He always said she did too much of that. That was one of her *many* problems.

The nurse continues, "Do you want to go on record saying this is a case of domestic violence? If so, we have to call the police. We're mandatory reporters. It's the law."

Her head spins. Déjà vu. Exactly how it ended for her parents. In an emergency room. It can't end that way for her. Besides, domestic violence is what happened to Nicole Brown Simpson. What happened to her was a mistake. An accident. In fact, now that she thinks about it, it must have been her fault. *"Did I just say that?"* she wonders. But only for a moment. Too many years in the House of Numb.

"It was an accident." She says finally.

The nurse looks relieved. Less paperwork. Less hassle. Less to think about.

She closes her tired eyes. *Bless me Father, for I have sinned.*

—May 25, 1997 The Tullahoma News

COLOR ME BLUE

Thanks to psychologists Ed and Carol Diener of the University of Illinois-Urbana, I am off the happiness hook. Nearly four decades of trying to rationalize my predominantly melancholic mood has been, well, depressing. Especially when the perpetrators are cheerful people. Those annoying, "have a nice day" sanguine types who seem immune to despair. You know who you are. So if the smug smile fits, skip this column and move on to the syrupy section. Fellow dysthymics, read on.

According to the Dieners' latest study, major stressors (e.g., the death of a loved one, divorce, unemployment) apparently do not permanently affect one's mood. In fact, within a year of experiencing a catastrophe, many people return to the mood they were in prior to the stressful event. That's supposed to be the good news.

The bad news, *aka* reality, is that studies are finding more and more evidence to support the theory that happiness, like weight, may have a genetically determined set point. Sure you can diet, but if you came assembled to resemble an A-frame house, forget it. A lifetime of lettuce lunches won't compensate for the girth gene. Same with happiness. Win the lottery tomorrow, but within six months, your misery-based DNA will return to its melancholic set point. Of course, you'll return first class. And you'll be miserable in a much classier neighborhood. But I digress…

Earlier research by psychologist David Meyers found that the number one predictor of happiness was being married to whom subjects described as their "best friend." Conversely, the most miserable were those married to their worst enemy. Which explains a lot. Like why there are more former than current spouses in my family. And why suicide is the leading cause of death in my family. A cheerful lot, we're not.

Thirty-seven years ago, my father made a single entry into my baby book. It foretold the future: "Subject (Dad liked the scientific approach) appears reluctant to walk at age one year. Fear and inability to concentrate seem to be the major causes. Subject can talk some. She is very persistent in each attempt to carry out her desires...subject is crafty, curious, high strung, and very nervous in general. Subject is very bright and aware of her environment to a remarkable degree. She is also destructive and has violent outbursts of emotions." He did not mention cheerful.

I have kept a journal since I was 13. Twenty-five years of recording dark, brooding thoughts. Inner turmoil. Anguish. Despair. Hopelessness. Revisiting the past through the lens of my moods is strangely comforting. My depression and I have been together forever. It's the one relationship that seems to last.

Now, thanks to the Dieners' findings, I can embrace my mood with the passion and commitment it deserves. No more ambivalence. I am liberated, at last, from the pretense of cheerfulness. No more self-imposed diets of low-calorie optimism. Horrible diets that leave me starved for melancholia. Intensity. Depth. Existential angst. My favorite and familiar demons. And demons they are. But slaying them would require sacrificing the angels, as well. So my moods and I have learned to co-exist without chemicals.

Life in a perpetual state of anomie means some days I write satire. Other days, I write about painful, intense topics. When truly miserable, I slit my wrists with my pen and allow the pain to flow through poetry. And there are days I do not write at all.

Several years ago, Pulitzer-prize winning author William Styron wrote an intense, compelling account of his struggle with depression. *Darkness Visible* is a story I wish I had the talent to tell. It's painful. Provocative. And deeply personal. Nothing a cheerful person could pen or comprehend.

Darkness Visible was required reading in both my Introductory and Abnormal Psychology courses. Three years in a row. Many intense classroom discussions about the causes, course, and cures for depression followed.

Once, a student asked my professional opinion of Prozac. I responded, "For some, it's been a life saver. For others, it's meant a life of beige. Normal."

Another student, sensing a story (he'd taken other classes with me and knew how to frame a question for maximum return) asked, "But what is your *personal* opinion?" I couldn't resist.

When I finished my story about the demons and angels, the room was silent. It was a powerful moment. Vivid. Very

Styronesque. Something the chronically cheerful will never experience. Vivid and beige do not mix.

The following week, I received several notes from students thanking me for speaking candidly about depression. One of my top students wrote, "when I was in high school, my parents had me hospitalized for six weeks because I was depressed. Until you spoke about depression, and the right to be intense, I felt like a total freak. Nobody ever told me it was okay not to be constantly cheerful. More importantly, nobody ever told me that it was okay to be me. Thank you for the new perspective."

Sound bizarre? Maybe. But only to the chronically happy. The beige. Those committed to quiet lives of desperate optimism.

So spread your cheer. But please understand, some of us like it dark. Intense. High impact.

Normal is relative. Beige. And beige is *not* my color.

—June 7, 1997 *The Dispatch*

RETURNING TO THE SCENE OF THE CRIME

October 8, 1992. I was returning to the scene of the crime: Moline. Men. Misery. Crimes of passion. Inextricably bound. And the reason I'd left in 1987. I would never return. Ever.

But that was before I met my own personal version of Bill Clinton. Ironically, the love of my complicated life lived in the very place I'd vowed never to return to. Deeply rooted in the local political milieu, he'd never leave the Quad-Cities. And I now live 600 miles away. Poetic justice.

There is a Chinese proverb that says the one who loves the least has the most power in a relationship. Which explains why, after a nearly six year stalemate, I finally packed my bags and headed home. Back to the past in search of a future.

Mohammed would not come to the mountain. So, the mountain moved to Moline. It was here or nowhere. Especially since I'd set my sights on becoming Hillary. Right down to my headband and boxed blonde coif. It was, after all, election year. Anything was possible.

The cerulean sky was cloudless that October day. The leaves, vibrant and colorful, were just days from their peak. The mild fall breeze did not yet pack the punch of the winter winds that slice through the Quad-Cities. Picture perfect weather. Eminently memorable because it was also the day I first met Dr. David Devonis.

"Do you read Russian literature?" inquired my prospective employer.

I stared blankly at the man seated across from me. "As if," I thought. I'm the first to admit I'm not the most scholarly person to ever stand in front of a student audience. At least not in the traditional sense of scholarship. But I do genuinely enjoy being around students. Debating ideas. Sharing their dreams and hopes. Helping with their struggles. Every student has a name and a story. And every student matters.

Russian literature. Just my luck. Of all the teaching joints in the world, I had to stumble into the one with a department chair who had a fetish for Tolstoy. An eccentric genius, no doubt. Dr. Devonis, that is.

I cursed myself for watching *Melrose Place* instead of PBS. Sleaze over substance. It was a serious character flaw.

As I silently berated myself, he opened a book and read aloud, "All happy families are alike; each unhappy family is different in its own way."—*Anna Karenina*. Leo Tolstoy's classic story of a dysfunctional family. "That," said the man who would eventually become both my boss and dear friend, "is psychology in a nutshell." Thus ended our interview. No mention of my teaching background, my career goals (or lack of), or my real agenda for showing up out of the blue at Marycrest University. All of that would come later.

He was big on metaphors. Imagery. And quirky historical anecdotes that provided students (and me) many hours of entertainment and enlightenment. The simple truth is that Dave loves to teach. The classroom is his natural habitat. The place where things make sense. And like me, Dave sincerely cares about every student who walks into his classroom.

He hired me the same day we met. In spite of my disinterest in Russian literature. Later, Dave told me that he'd seen potential in me. An earlier version of himself. In short, he believed in me long before I believed in me.

As I walked down the hall that day, he called out to me. "I hope you find whatever it is that brought you back here." The genius was also perceptive.

And so it began. Dave and I went on to co-teach classes, co-author papers and collaborate on numerous other professional endeavors. He was my mentor, but more importantly, Dave blessed me with his friendship. And his ongoing faith in my ability to make something out of myself.

This summer, I took a break from journalism so we could teach one last class together at Marycrest. In September, Dave will begin a new teaching assignment at a small liberal arts college in Lamoni, Iowa.

After our final class, we spent several hours reflecting on the rewards and challenges of the classroom. In the end, we realized, it's not about us. It's about the students we send out of the classroom, hopefully, a little more informed and aware. A little less overwhelmed by the complexities of life. And in a better position to face the demands of life outside the classroom.

"A mind once stretched can never return to its original dimensions," observed Oliver Wendell Holmes. That's what teaching is all about. Stretching a mind. Making room for new possibilities. And ultimately, making a difference.

As for my fairy tale, the jury is still out. The dream that drove me 600 miles back to my past still lingers in my heart. He still lives in Moline. And I now live 700 miles away. But as Scarlett said, "Tomorrow is another day."

In the meantime, turn out the lights when you leave, Dave. And may you find the life you hoped for. You were the best boss a misplaced woman could ever find.

—August 13, 1997 *The Dispatch*

Author's Note: I was a visiting lecturer at Teikyo Marycrest University from January, 1993 thru December, 1995, when I returned to Tennessee. For the next two years, I would travel back to the QC periodically so Dave and I could co-teach a class. Marycrest finally closed in 1998.

Now at Graceland University, Dave still teaches psychology.

REMEMBERING MY ROYAL SOULMATE

On the surface, we had nothing in common. It is highly unlikely that we would ever have had occasion to cross paths. We hardly traveled in the same circles.

Unlike the rest of the world, I did not vicariously attend the wedding of the century. I was not impressed with the prince. Nor was I fascinated with Diana's apparent fairy tale lifestyle. Until the day our vastly different lives intersected in the strangest of ways.

December, 1992. I was in the car, driving back to Moline from Nashville. My then two-year-old daughter and I were on our way to my mother's. My marriage was over. We were now officially separated. I was completely disoriented. Lost. And terrified. I know I should have seen it coming. Fairy tales do not go awry overnight. But denial is a powerful deterrent to the truth.

Throughout the 600-mile trip, I switched radio stations a dozen times, hoping to find some direction in the music. That afternoon, speeding through Kentucky, I first heard the news announcement from Buckingham Palace that Charles and Diana were officially separating. So, two marriages a world apart, were coming to the same unhappy ending on the same dreary December day. Now I was mildly interested. Misery loves company.

Over the next few years, I became fascinated with Diana's story. Not the glamorous façade. The wealth. Or even the incredible power she seemed capable of wielding. I was intrigued by the incredible losses Diana had sustained throughout her life. The self-doubt that plagued her. The "emotional confusion." And the depression that she struggled with. In so many ways, Diana seemed like me with a crown. Including a record four year marital separation.

Across the miles and misery, my royal soulmate (as she became) was faring no better in her personal life than I was. We each lived in a special kind of hell, neither married nor officially divorced.

Our respective marriages had died in much the same way. A quiet death of indifference. A clash in style. The fairy tale gone awry. We did our time in marital limbo. Lonely. And chronically misunderstood. Ironically, I realized, for many of the same reasons.

Neither of us wanted to return to pre-career wife life. Both of us had married up and wanted to hold on to at least a piece of the fairy tale. And, more than anything, we both wanted a happy ending. So, while others divorced and remarried, we hung on to our respective illusions. We ate our lettuce lunches. We worked out. We focused on being mothers. We searched for lasting love. And we were always camera-ready. The jet set circle of the elite. The suburbs of Hollywood South. The distance isn't really so far. Loss is loss. Pain is pain. And eventually, it comes to every zip code.

After Diana's divorce became final last August, I stopped keeping up with her. She had been released from her personal prison. I still had time to do. But I wished her well. I hoped she'd get that elusive second chance for a happy ending. And I pressed on alone, hoping my own freedom would soon follow.

Recently, I caught a clip on CNN showing Diana and her companion, Dodi Fayed beginning their second European vacation in less than a month. I smiled to myself and silently wished I could be her. She was free. She had found love, at last. And she was getting her second chance for a happy ending. So it looked.

Today the world grieves over the death of a woman everyone knew of, but few actually knew. And even fewer understood. In the days to come, there will be accusations and blame. Celebrities will sound outraged and commiserate about the parasite photographers who stalk them relentlessly. The media will defend its right to pursue those in the public eye. Politicians will make statements of sympathy. Both commoners and royals will grieve. The innumerable lives Diana touched will be forever changed. And columnists will struggle with words to make sense of a senseless tragedy.

In the end, Diana died the way she lived. In the fast lane. And in search of love. Perhaps her search ended with Fayed. Maybe she did indeed get that second chance. If only for a moment. We'll never know. But one thing is certain: she kept her promise. In death, as well as life, she did not go quietly.

—September 3, 1997 *The Tullahoma News*
—September 7, 1997 *The Dispatch*

THIS WIFE FOR HIRE

Nine marriage proposals. Four fiancés. Two decades of dating. One and a half bad marriages. And now another birthday looming on the horizon. Thirty-nine. It's enough to make you stop and think. Especially when you're staring down the face of forty as a single woman.

During times like this, columnists often feel compelled to share their vast insights on the human condition. Weigh in on some lofty existential dilemma. Debate the issue of the day. Not me. I've decided, at long last, to bring to bear the power of the press to accomplish something truly impressive—find a date for Saturday night.

To paraphrase Leslie Gore, "It's my column, and I'll cry if I want."

Times are tough. Trust me. I'm out there on the front lines. And frankly, I'd rather stick my head in a bag of broken glass than go out on one more first date. But I digress.

The purpose of today's column is to help me find a man like Nathan Hauser. Nathan is bright, good-looking, sincere, stable, and completely faithful to his girlfriend. I know, because his girlfriend is my daughter.

They're both six-years-old. Nearly seven. And they've been inseparable since they were 2½. Which is three years longer than any of my relationships ever lasted. Even more amazing, they live 700 miles apart and only see each other during our summer sabbaticals to Moline, and for a few weeks in October. Still, Nathan remains totally smitten with my daughter.

This summer, I took the lovebirds to the Fourth of July parade in East Moline. Nova sang, *Don't Cry For Me Argentina* six times between Nathan's house and the parade. A pint-sized Evita...

Did Nathan complain? Tell her to shut up? Interrupt? Not a peep. In spite of the fact that she rather abruptly informed him that she won't ever marry him, unless, "you become Juan Peron when you grow up."

My daughter wants to marry a dictator. And I'm still looking for the prince. Freud would be amused. After all, it was he who asked (but never answered), "What do women want?"

The answer is simple. We want a pulse. Everything else is elective. Like most men, Freud didn't get it.

So what exactly is this jaded Cinderella looking for? Not much, actually. Just a kindred spirit who gets the drift. Someone who will listen patiently to my brooding thoughts, pander to my neurotic ego, and cater to my mood swings. Don't worry. I'll do the same for you. I was married for ten years. I've had plenty of baby-sitting experience.

A Neiman-Marcus credit card with a high line limit and a solid dental plan round out my meager expectations. No humor-impaired Republicans. And no creatively-challenged conformists. Must be willing to live on the edge. And dream big. The Beltway beckons.

What's in it for you? A woman who considers Victoria's Secret a source of career apparel. A woman you can take home—even to meet mom. A woman who knows the difference between monogamy and monotony. A woman who realizes self-respect is overrated. At the very least, I'm never boring. Ask any of my exes. "Life with you is a life on Rolaids," fiancé number three often complained. But he never mentioned boring.

"You frighten people—me especially," whined fiancé number four, after a harmless prank went slightly awry. So electricity and water don't mix. Who knew? At least he was out of the hospital in less time than it takes to say, "charge it." Which due to an unfortunate computer error, he can no longer do. Seems he's been a victim of identity theft. When it rains, it pours.

So there you have it. Chronically misunderstood, but highly creative wife for hire in search of a psychologically-minded prince. If you're out there—or if you're eligible for parole soon, send your complete salary history, social security number, and mother's maiden name to Fairy Tales, Inc. in care of this newspaper. Or stop by. If it's a slow news day, you might get an interview. Quotes from princes and paroled politicians make for great copy. Meanwhile, I hope you show up soon. I could use a happy ending. And a trip to Neiman-Marcus. Mall withdrawal is not a pretty sight.

—October 27, 1997 *The Dispatch*

POWER SHOPPING FOR ABSOLUTION

My daughter has a long list of things she *must* have for Christmas. Toys (with a zillion small pieces). Games. Dolls. Clothes. And more toys. Lots of tangible goods. All the usual longings of childhood.

As I peruse Nova's list, I am struck by the simplicity of it. She believes the things on her list will make her happy. And thanks to the mental myopia that protects most children from the crushing disappointment of reality, her illusion will remain intact. For at least a few more years. And, then, like the rest of us, she will learn the painful truth; no mall on Earth sells absolution.

No amount of money can bring someone back from the dead, buy good health, or restore lost innocence. Money cannot change life's course by undoing that fatal left turn or reversing a catastrophic mistake. Nor can money buy love that endures. In fact, money can slowly poison love, turning it into a hideous greedy monster that feeds on everything but the truth. Until it dies an agonizing death.

Money can't stop the pain, either. I should know. I've spent most of my adult life worshipping at the altar of Neiman-Marcus. A plastic princess power shopping for absolution. Preferably on the clearance rack. In basic black, size two. Something that can be worn from dinner to death. Something like redemption.

Sadly, we must learn the hard way that aging, loneliness, loss and death will still come, even to the best-dressed neighborhoods. Worse, money can't buy the family or the Kodak moments we dream of. Someone else got that life, and it's simply not for sale.

At the mall, clocks are not allowed to be displayed in public view. The reason is simple: money can't stop time. Visa may be everywhere you want to be, but it can't turn the clock back. Tomorrow and all its uncertainty will come, regardless of socioeconomic status. Wealth and worth are not the same.

No amount of money can truly quiet the heart. Inspire the imagination. Soothe a lost soul. Or buy enough faith to face the future without fear. And it certainly can't buy forgiveness. Or even second chances.

The phone call or visit to grandma that we didn't have time to make. The letter we never got around to writing. Words from the heart that were never expressed. Or even the pedestrian parenting activities that were forever postponed: the board game there was never enough time to play, or the silly requests to "play dress-up with me" or "give me a piggyback ride" that went ignored. They are moments forever lost.

So, we head to the mall, like sacrificial lambs to slaughter, in search of salvation. Especially during this time of the year. We just can't let Christmas off the hook. We expect more miracles from this one poor holiday than it can ever realistically deliver.

Our shopping lists are lengthy and labored: Fractured families will get fixed. The statute of limitations will run out on old grudges. Happy endings will replace unhappy beginnings. Everyone at the dinner table will cheerfully offer a hug and a kind word in place of the usual acrimony. Restraining orders will not be served before dinner. Tawdry gifts and tacky spouses will be a thing of the past. And for once in his life, Uncle Joe will arrive in a dinner jacket rather than a verbal straitjacket (now *who* still believes in Santa Claus?).

We seem destined to watch helplessly as our hopes and dreams collapse under the weight of reality. Can't get no satisfaction, as the song goes. Yet, we still search—and shop relentlessly, for that elusive happy ending. And retailers are happy to oblige. Guilt is a great marketing tool. Unfortunately, it's also false advertising. We all know who has the market cornered on guilt. And He does not accept credit cards. Platinum or otherwise.

So, I'm going back to my daughter's list. It's a lot easier to navigate. In the meantime, my wish for you is simple: May you be blessed with a quiet heart, love that lasts, and the vision to follow your dreams. And may your journey take you to undiscovered places of the heart. With no line limit. And lots of happy endings.

Sorry, no refunds or exchanges. All wishes are final.

—December 24, 1997 *The Huntsville Times*

THE GHOST OF NEW YEARS' PAST

Have you ever chased a ghost? Elusive (but oh, so seductive), the ghosts of a past imperfect are sly creatures.

And very nimble. One minute they're just within our grasp. The next minute they've scattered in the wind, escaping our best laid plans to defeat them. And then, just when we least expect them, they return to haunt and taunt us with their presence. Always threatening to disappear on a whim with what remains of our dignity. Or worse, to stay and remind us constantly of our flaws and foibles: Excess weight. Wrinkles. Smoking. Laziness. Procrastination. Poor self-confidence. Apathy. Chronic loneliness. Crushing boredom. General life dissatisfaction.

We either chase or are chased relentlessly by our favorite ghosts. It is a familiar dance between partners of the past and present. The perennial diet dances with the lack of willpower. The long-suffering spouse dances with low self-esteem. Passion dances with pain. Intimacy dances with indifference. Success, and its twin ghost, Failure, dance a complicated rumba across the workplace, straight into our homes, and eventually come to rest deep in our troubled hearts.

Ghosts always win. We are, after all, only human. But we remain intrigued by their folly—and motivated by their magic. If we could just catch (and conquer) our ghosts, perhaps we could have a piece of their magic. And life would be good. Maybe even thrilling.

So, every New Years Day, we arm ourselves with our favorite ghost-buster: a list of New Year's resolutions. And then we prepare to do battle with some formidable opponents. Lose weight. Quit smoking. Get organized. Find a soulmate. Get a life. All the usual ghosts that escaped last year. And the year before.

But this year will be different (translation: better), we promise ourselves with the conviction of a Branch Dividian. A clean slate. New tactics. And renewed enthusiasm to conquer our ghosts. We will win this year, we promise ourselves.

And thus begins the dance of despair: what's eating us, we finally realize, is bigger than what we eat. It's nearly impossible to be both happy and healthy at the same time. That's why Freud's couch was never empty. Neurosis, not ignorance, is the key to bliss. Nice and numb is a lot easier and less complicated than intense and intimate. The flight from insight is already overbooked. And most of the passengers are those who have the misfortune to love. Worse, it's a one-way flight.

Open-ended grief remains open-ended pain. Limbo (the preferred venue for dead relationships) is just another name for hell. Everyone has an agenda. Some people even have a flair for despair. Others are happy in an emotional junkyard. And even happier to have company. Yours.

We know these truisms about life and other difficult situations, yet we make our list of resolutions and check them twice. As if we can really beat these ghosts from the past and present that torment us. The past, as Faulkner noted, is never dead. It's not even in the past. It's not further than a glance in the mirror. The enemy, unfortunately, is us. And our impossible resolutions.

Perhaps a healthier (and wiser) course of action would be to simply make peace with our feared, yet familiar ghosts. Instead of making a list of all the things we need to change, maybe we should be compiling a list of all the things we need to keep the same. All the things that we like about ourselves. The things we've done right. The simple things that make us unique. Lovable. Memorable. And poignantly human.

It would, admittedly, be a shorter list for most of us. But it would be a more realistic list. A true ghost-buster. And a far more forgiving way to begin the new year.

Or, make it even simpler. Instead of resolutions, make reservations. At a great restaurant. And order double dessert. Preferably something chocolate and gooey. One for you. And one for the ghost of diets past. And then have a Happy New Years. Ghosts and all.

—January 2, 1998 *The Tullahoma News*

LOVE, MARRIAGE, AND INDICTMENTS

L ast year, Tennessee became one of the few states in the nation to allow residents to carry a concealed weapon. Although merely a technicality (gun racks are standard equipment on most trucks sold in Tennessee), the new concealed weapon law does remind men that in these parts, women still take long-term relationships seriously. A woman who carries both a Luger and lipstick in her handbag is not easily ignored.

Down here, life is simple. We don't stand on formality. Unless it involves marriage. Which, I should point out to my Yankee readers (namely, my last four fiancés), is a given after either the third date or sex. Whichever comes first. To avoid trouble, just follow this simple rule of thumb: the first date indicates interest; a second date implies intentions; a third date means you're planning to set the date. Don't worry, by the third date, you'll know her whole family. Intimately. Including those on work-release. Your new best friends are her burly-looking brothers and cousins who spend their days discussing family honor and the "war of northern aggression." Now is not the time to crack that joke about Sherman being the father of modern urban renewal. Trust me.

In the South, divorce is often deadly because of the one principle that drives our culture: blood is thicker than water, money is thicker than blood, and honor is thickest of all. This basic truism applies to everything important. Family feuds. Funerals. And flings.

Just one more difference between North and South. Up North, marriages usually end in civil court. Here, marriages tend to end in criminal court. With at least one spouse under indictment. What else do you expect in an area with more churches and escort services per capita than any other region in the U.S.? Relationships matter to us.

However, the relationship-challenged can be found here, too. Everywhere from the trailer park to the Mayor's office. For example, in 1991, our then mayor, Bill Boner, had the rare distinction of being both married and engaged at the same time. Not one to pass up an opportunity to self-disclose on national television, Boner proudly defended both his arrangement and his honor on *The Phil Donahue Show*... Later, when it was more economically feasible, he divorced. Married. Divorced. And remarried. A total of five times. Then, during a recent election year conversion, Boner found religion and lost the women. We forgave him. And elected him to the state General Assembly.

Divorce was also a disaster for my neighbors Betty Jean and Bubba. Particularly, Betty Jean, who like most of us, hasn't had a paying job since she said, "I do." Where does a woman who thinks Internet is a new hairspray go to find work? And what about her ten children? All under the age of thirteen. Sure, the oldest two will be getting married soon (no, not to each other—that's East Tennessee), but that still leaves the other eight. Then there's poor Bubba. He hasn't had any real peace of mind since the day he accidentally wandered into the new HOV lane on I-65 ("I can't believe they done built a special lane for homosexuals.") after Betty Jean told him she "wanted some space."

And then there's Sue Ann. At a recent church barbecue, she quietly announced that her husband is divorcing her. Seems he's fallen in love with a salesgirl at the local Christian bookstore.

After a long, awkward silence, my friend, Wanda, offered her condolences. "Bless your heart, darlin'. What *will* you do?"

Another strained silence. Sue Ann didn't answer. She didn't have to. We all knew the dreadful truth. She would have to get a job. As in work. It was a death sentence. Rock bottom. The end of the designer line.

The next day, while standing in line to renew my license plates, I overhear two women behind the counter discussing Sue Ann's property settlement with the woman in line ahead of me (down here, gossip is an art form). It seems Bill (Sue Ann's soon-to-be ex) is demanding an expensive family heirloom—an armoire—in the property settlement. The armoire, according to Wilma (so the nameplate on her chest says), was Sue Ann's grandmother's. How tacky. "Does that man have no sense of honor?" Wilma asks her co-worker and those of us standing in line.

"He's from California," offers the well-dressed woman in front of me.

"Oh good Lord—that explains it. Them mixed marriages never work out."

While stamping my paperwork, Wilma's co-worker phones her source to verify that Bill is indeed trying to finagle the armoire.

"Myrtle says it's true. Sure enough."

Getting my car tags renewed in Moline was never this informative. Or eventful. But then neither were my relationships (not to be mistaken for "dates).

As I leave, I notice a funeral procession going down the road. It is a short line. Probably somebody from out of state. Maybe Bill. He obviously has a death wish. And he clearly doesn't know the rules. Very tacky. And very deadly.

—November 7, 1997 *The Tullahoma News*
—February 13, 1998 *The Dispatch*

THE WINDFALL THAT WASN'T

My favorite aunt telephoned recently with exciting news—she'd won money in the California lottery.

My pulse raced. I held my breath. Was my decidedly working-class existence about to accelerate into the affluent lane? I was after all, her favorite niece. I always remember Aunt Corinne on her birthday. Okay—it's the day after my own birthday, but technicalities don't matter where windfalls are concerned. Besides, I write my aunt regularly. And I send pictures of all family events. She always says it means a lot to her. I *am* a good niece, I reminded myself with the conviction of a zealot.

Now the cosmos would reward me. All those deposits of good-will at the Bank of Karma were about to pay off. I just knew it.

"One hundred dollars," she gushed with the same enthusiasm exhibited by $10,000,000 winners facing Ed McMahon on live television. Aunt Corinne then proceeded to tell me how she spent her sudden largesse: lunch at a sit down restaurant, a trinket for my daughter, a minor car repair, and of course, more lottery tickets. Mundane purchases for an equally pedestrian lifestyle, I sulked. My flight of fancy had just crashed and burned far short of the suburbs. There was no escape from the black hole of reality.

The rest of our conversation focused on work. Hers. My aunt is the only person I know who truly likes her job. And what is her high-powered, glamorous career? She works in a factory just outside Los Angeles. Sewing pieces of fabric into tablecloths. Six days a week. From 6 A.M. until 3 P.M.

Even more amazing than job satisfaction, she also likes—no, loves—the rest of her life. For example, on the morning of the most recent measurable earthquake in L.A., my aunt arrived at work only twenty minutes late. She apologized to her supervisor and went straight to work on making tablecloths. L.A. was trembling violently, on the verge of becoming an island headed for Asia, and my aunt was concerned only that she was twenty minutes late for a job that pays approximately $10 an hour. How is this possible?

Anything that smacks of contentment is viewed with suspicion by my generation. We are an unhappy lot. Compulsively driven. Neurotic. And almost genetically incapable of experiencing anything that remotely resembles contentment. Which makes people like my aunt an anomaly. And therefore, the first of my relatives to rank an entire column. I want to know her secret. Maybe readers can help me out…

In the meantime, I've been thinking about what grandiose (read: superior) things I would have done with the windfall that wasn't. As a former therapist, I have asked many clients the question, "What do you really want?" Now it was my turn to generate a list of things that would make me happy.

My list included such items as seeing my father again (he died when I was a teenager), a home (and a family to go with it), true love, and everyone's favorite: more time. Pulitzer Prize optional.

After finishing my wish list, I was surprised to discover that in actuality, I had compiled a list of the top reasons why winning the lottery, or any sweepstakes, could never fix this mess we call reality. It was a sobering moment.

No amount of money can bring someone back from the dead, buy good health, or restore lost innocence. Money cannot change life's course by undoing that fatal left turn or reversing a catastrophic mistake. Money cannot buy love that endures. In fact, lust for money—and the power that accompanies affluence—often destroys love. Ask any celebrity.

Money definitely can't stop the pain. Aging, loneliness, loss, and death will still come, even to the best zip codes. Money can't buy the family or the Kodak moments we dream of. Someone else got that life and it's not for sale.

Money can't stop time. Tomorrow and all its uncertainty will come regardless of socioeconomic status. No amount of money can truly quiet a heart. Inspire the imagination. Soothe a lost soul. Or buy enough faith to face the future without fear. And it certainly can't buy my aunt's enthusiasm for life.

On the other hand, let's be practical. An unexpected windfall would at least allow one to be miserable in a classier neighborhood. So, pass the Prozac and count me in for a lottery ticket.

—March 20, 1998 *The Tullahoma News*

NO WILL, NO WAY

'*For the best view of your life, climb your family tree*" Robert Noone (U.S. Catholic, 1988).

Six aunts and uncles. Five cousins. All four grandparents. Three former bosses. Two boyfriends. One brother. One parent. A bunch of acquaintances. No partridge in a pear tree.

Death. You'd think I'd be used to it. By age 23, I had attended the funerals of my dad, brother, three grandparents, a former boyfriend, and one uncle. By age 35, the rest were gone. Needless to say, it has given me a different perspective on many issues.

Black is my color. And often, my mood. Accessorized with chronic grief. I seem to wear it well. Practice makes perfect, they say. One more thing I have in common with my Beltway hero, dubbed mourner-in-chief who, during an interview with Barbara Walters, once remarked that he had no idea "this job would involve so many funerals."

So much loss. And still so little understanding of that thief in the night that claims our infants and elderly alike. The healthy and the chronically ill. The good. The evil. The rich. And the poor. Death eventually comes to every zip code. It is the ultimate non-partisan event.

Last year, one of my aunts died suddenly. She had never married. No children. Little property. Few assets. And no will. She never got around to it. She didn't think she had anything of value.

The family feeding frenzy that followed proved her wrong. Since Joyce had no immediate family, her siblings (both living and deceased), became the heirs to her estate. Under Tennessee law, the children of the deceased siblings become heirs to their parent's portion of the estate.

Suddenly, I was on "the list" (my father was her brother). My two half-brothers, half-sister, and seven cousins (children of the other deceased siblings) were also included on the list. The surviving siblings were not happy about the list.

Our family motto is simple: blood is thicker than water, but money is thicker than anything. Any threat to this credo activates the grudge gene (a dominant family trait). Scores are kept and settled. Alliances shift. Unspoken rules, bad tempers, and on-going vendettas make every family event an exercise in high drama. Death included.

In every family, however, there is an exception. In ours, it's the family patriarch, Walter Gillespie. He got the single recessive integrity gene. When Uncle Walter stepped forward and assumed responsibility for the disbursement of Joyce's meager monetary estate, he made sure every relative on the list received an equal share.

With integrity at the helm, there might have been a happy ending to this particular episode of family feud had Aunt Norma Bates not emerged from the family shower and her latest lawsuit long enough to confiscate the one valuable personal possession Joyce did have— our family history. Eighteen photo albums full.

Joyce's picture-taking hobby was something we all took for granted. For nearly fifty years, she had painstakingly photographed every rogue relative, shirttail cousin, and short-term spouse that had graced our family with their pathetically normal presence. The sane do not linger in our family. Still, all the bit players and family stars have been captured on Kodak paper at least once by our family photographer. The result is a sprawling pictorial history of four generations of a large, traditional Southern family.

Some of the photos were of my dad. He died when I was fifteen. My first death. But far from the last.

Today, I have only one picture of the man who taught me about the stars, defended my honor to the boys in the neighborhood, stood behind me, and believed in me. Just one picture of the man who loved me first and most. And frankly, it's looking rough. Too much wear and tear. Too many tears spilled over it.

In an attic across town, there are dozens more. But I will never see them. No will. No way. That's the law. Or lack of.

Wills are synonymous with a lot of things we'd prefer to ignore—namely our mortality. I can still remember agonizing for nearly three years over which of my friends to choose as Nova's legal guardian in the event of my death. Suddenly, my wonderful friends all seemed fatally flawed in some way. Every one of them failed to "measure up" to my expectations of stand-in parent for my precious offspring. Either they're atheists or flaming fundamentalists. They smoke. They're Republicans. They have bad taste in clothes. They eat weird food. They believe in babysitters. They have other children. They spank. They're too permissive. They have the wrong color hair. In short, they just aren't me. The perfect parent for my daughter.

Still, wills are the last, best way to say goodbye to those we care about. So, I finally bit the bullet and chose Nova's godmother for the job. It was the right thing to do. And a choice I can live with. Hopefully for many years to come.

As for the rest of the family, the legacy of revenge continues. Without me. My will be done.

—February 22, 1998 *The Tullahoma News*
—March 31, 1998 *The Dispatch*

MOTHER'S DAY CARDS FOR
DYSFUNCTIONAL FAMILIES

Another Mother's Day. Second only to Christmas on the Chronic Disappointment Index, Mother's day serves as an annual reminder to those of us who never quite measured up in the daughter department of how cruel genetics can be. And how Hallmark-challenged we are.

For example, where are the Mother's Day cards with realistic sentiments like, "Okay, I'm not the perfect daughter—but at least I'm not under indictment this year" or "Please accept this card in lieu of a gift...all my money goes for therapy. And how's your life, Mommie dearest?"

For the more poetic-minded, "Roses are red, violets are blue, I don't know you and you don't know me, but if you don't return my real mom, we're both dead." Mother's Day cards for dysfunctional families.

Even better would be a generic one-size-fits-all maternal disappointment card. Suitable for framing, it would read something like this:

Dear Mom: First, there was the matter of my childhood. Constantly colluding with dad to keep your life simmering on slow boiling misery was clearly an unpardonable crime. A little geography and a lot of time have gone a long way toward emotional parole. For both of us.

Second, there was the unfortunate tragedy of adolescence. Mine. Growing up Catholic, I blindly conformed to the official party line (of both parenting and parochial school): "If we want your opinion, we'll give it to you." Yes sister, yes ma'am.

All went well until the hormones from hell kicked in and transformed an angel into an attitude on heels. And then came boys. It went downhill from there.

My twenties were characterized by a state of chronic disbelief. Yours.

Convinced there had been some mix-up at the hospital two decades earlier, you decided to correct the "mistake" through an exercise in sheer will. Trying to mold your misguided offspring into an acceptable daughter was the real mistake. One of the few things we have in common is willfulness. So began the war of two women.

Twenty years older and wiser, you finally realize the daughter you dreamed of is not going to show up. And to your credit, you've come to accept this sad truism.

Little more than familiar strangers who happen to share the same gene pool, we have worked hard to forge a friendship. The path has not been easy. For either of us. But it continues to be an effort that must be made. Family is way too important to dismiss because of differences. No matter how strident.

Like a lot of mothers and daughters, we're as different as night and day. And, had we not been related, I doubt we would have ever met. We travel in different circles. Way different circles.

You were a career woman long before there was such a term. A homeowner at twenty-eight, you'd been in the workforce full-time for more than twenty years by the time you reached my age. I have yet to have a full-time job (as you constantly remind me) or to stay in one place more than a few years. Creative people tend to be restless souls. And we stay in perpetual motion.

You're also fiercely independent when it comes to men. I'm not. Your favorite response (read: directive) to my post-divorce whine was simply, "learn to stand on your own two feet, Shalynn. Stop depending on men."

No tea and sympathy.

Admittedly, my life has been mostly defined by my relationships. Typical 90s woman—1890s. Somebody's daughter. Somebody's wife. Somebody's mother. Somebody's ex-wife. Somebody's soon-to-be wife.

You, by contrast, are nobody's somebody. You're your own person. I've always admired that aspect of your personality. Just like I admire Hillary Clinton. Not that I have anything in common with Hillary or will ever be like her. Still, I've always appreciated a good mystery. And from where I'm coming from, both you and Hillary are a mystery.

This year, we finally have a major life event in common. Divorce. The tie that binds. But not for long. I will remarry. Sooner rather than later. Still looking for rings and strings. Attachments. Family. And forever.

In the meantime, Happy Mother's Day. Thanks for putting your life on the line so I could have one, too. To paraphrase Mark Twain's revelation about his father, "the older you get, the more you seem to know." Hopefully, you also know that I love you. Differences and all.

—May 10, 1998 *The Dispatch*

LOST AND LIVING IN NORMANDY

One year ago today, I first arrived in Normandy, Tennessee, population 141. The accidental tourist. The perennial tourist. The stranded tourist. All of these were—are—me.

I am, admittedly, still disoriented. Normandy is a long, long way from Hollywood South (aka Nashville) in all the ways that matter. Culturally. Emotionally. And spiritually. Which is good for Normandy, but confusing to civilians from the city.

The first shock occurred at the mall in nearby Tullahoma (population, a whopping 18,000). Spoiled by concrete cities like Hickory Hollow and Cool Springs Galleria that feature zillions of everything, I was not prepared for Northgate Mall. Especially when, after glancing at the sale flier I held out to him, the shoe salesman at the one anchor store said, "Sorry, we only got that shoe in a black, size 8. If you need a size 6, you'll have to take the red." Great. I did not want red. And definitely not a size 8.

Restricted selection, constricted lifestyle, I grumbled.

Next came the shock of familiarity. When I appeared in person at the water department to pay my first bill and a pleasant-looking cashier politely volunteered the history of the house I was renting, I was stunned silent. She knew my landlord, the area, and the history. And now, she knew me.

In Nashville, I never knew my next door neighbors, much less the history of the 'hood. In fact, I preferred *not* to know any more than I had to. Ignorance is bliss. Anonymity is even better.

"You live *past* the end of the earth," observed a friend visiting from St. Louis. "You're in exile," laughed a former editor. "I hope you're prepared to live in obscurity." A writer's worst nightmare. And I wasn't laughing.

Then came summer. Hot. Humid. Endless. And the beginning of yet another life lesson: If you're going to live in the country, it's always going to be man against nature. And guess who invariably wins?

A herd of deer feasted on my tomato plants. And my habanero peppers. Which was either incredibly brave or wildly stupid. Rabbits and other nocturnal critters ate the leftovers. Finally, only a large patch of barren garden remained.

Bumblebees larger than my thumb forced me to rethink the idea of hanging out the wash. Looking like escapees from the set of a horror movie, the insects from hell clearly carried a dominant gene for aggression. And a short temper. Which is why I quickly admitted defeat and resigned myself to a summer spent indoors.

Still, there was no escape. First it was the mice. They had come in undetected through an opening in the fireplace and taken up residence. And they had taken a shine to my baking. Chocolate connoisseurs, the little pests had come to the right house. A plate of chocolate cake here. A platter of chocolate chunk cookies there. It was rodent heaven. And I was slowly starving.

Finally, I did what all bleeding heart liberal Democrats do— blamed it on their environment. I had unintentionally tempted them with chocolate confections. I was responsible. And it was up to me to rehabilitate them. So, I set out humane traps and dutifully walked each furry inmate out to the adjacent barn and set him free with a stern warning not to return. It was a second chance at freedom. And a supreme exercise in stupidity. Mine.

Usually, they were back at the house before me. And back to their old ways. Recidivists. Finally, my landlord said *he* would take care of the mice. And that's the last I saw of them.

As summer faded into autumn, I thought I was finally learning to survive in the country. Until the morning I woke up at 4 A.M. with watery eyes and a wretched cough. A pungent odor had filled every room of my house. I knew that smell—skunk. Half asleep, half gagging, I figured the skunk had been hit by a car on the nearby road and the smell would soon dissipate. I was wrong.

The stinking scene of the crime was actually much closer. Under the crawl space of my house. And, because it was still stifling hot, the air conditioning had circulated Eau de Skunk throughout the house with remarkable efficiency. The stench remained for weeks.

Mercifully, winter passed uneventfully. And now spring has arrived. Meaning another round of man vs. nature. This year, I'm prepared. I'm spending the summer on the road. Ahead of the insects. And still in search of steppin' out, strappy shoes. Size 6. Black. Preferably on sale.   —May 19, 1998 *The Huntsville Times*

MY NAME IS SHALYNN,
AND I'M A CHOCOHOLIC

Hello. My name is Shalynn and I'm an addict. I blame my mother (hey, she's used to it. Besides, in this case, it's true—she's the one who first introduced her impressionable toddler to Homer Jackson's addictive double chocolate cake donuts after Sunday Mass). St. Mary's and Mello-Cream Donuts. Confession and confections. Sinfully sweet Sundays. The nice and the naughty. Inextricably bound.

Every Sunday after Mass (we often left immediately after Communion to get a jump start on traffic), we'd follow the scent of sugar straight down Fifth Avenue to Mello-Cream. Rows of perfectly formed, generously iced, deliciously doughy creations beckoned seductively from the store window. Freezer drawers held zillions more. Sugar nirvana.

It was a sad day for Moline when Homer closed his donut shop. And a sadder day still when the cherubic little guy passed away (taking along his recipes to the great pastry shop in the sky, no doubt). Homer and his donuts were a culinary institution that distinguished Moline from the rest of the Quad Cities pack. And the basis for some of my best Moline memories.

Fortunately, Moline still has Lagomarcino's for an unbeatable chocolate candy fix and Whitey's for ice cream that borders on a peak experience. In fact, Lago's and Whitey's are dangerous. They deal in pleasures of the palate. The kind you'd do unspeakable things to procure—if you had to. Which brings me to the point of today's column. Just how far would you go for a piece of chocolate? This is not a trick question.

According to reliable sources, including my boyfriend (an investigative reporter), three fellow panic-stricken junkies, and my mother (also one of the aforementioned junkies), there is an impending chocolate shortage. Something about production shortfall. Demand way exceeding supply. And possible market manipulation (drug dealers are all alike—always trying to drive up the price by cutting back on production). World-wide withdrawal. As in cut-off. Global cold turkey. Haagen-Dazs hell. A future sans chocolate. And you thought Saddam was a problem…

Just imagine a world without Mocha Cappuccino Fudge Swirl Ice Cream. Or Chocolate Chaos Cookies (my own secret recipe—to obtain a copy, send a self-addressed stamped envelope and $2.7 million dollars or the equivalent lifetime supply of Godiva truffles—no nuts—to me in care of this newspaper. Satisfaction guaranteed). Or even the pedestrian pleasure of mainlining a Hershey bar in times of trouble. It's not a pretty sight.

Ironically, several years ago, I predicted this very scenario. At the time, I was teaching Abnormal Psychology. When the discussion turned to various types of substance abuse, several students offered painful accounts of addictive experiences. Others, however, seemed a little too smug about their drug-free lifestyle. Self-righteous indignation rearing its ugly head. So, I decided to "come out." Share my darkest (fudge) secret.

I'm an addict, I told them. The same as an alcoholic. The only difference is that my drug of choice is legal. It's not sanctioned by society. And it's readily available. But what if it weren't, I asked my skeptical students.

Initially, they had a hard time comprehending the parallels between cocaine and chocolate addiction. Until I explained that numerous studies have found that the mechanism of addiction is identical. The same area of the brain lights up like a Christmas tree when stimulated with either substance. And, like most addicts, it appears laboratory rats are willing to die for chocolate. For example, when offered rewards of either cocaine or chocolate, the furry junkies sat in their cages and bar pressed with such rapidity and vigor that they eventually overdosed and died. Satiated but dead. Just for an Oreo. They probably didn't even get a glass of milk with their poison. They definitely didn't get sex. Sleep. Or exercise. They sacrificed it all in the name of Godiva.

"So," I told my students, "as long as there's plenty of chocolate, no one gets hurt." But, what if chocolate were suddenly illegal? How far would you go for a fix?

Petty theft? Turning tricks downtown? Exchanging favors for flavors? An internship at the White House? A twelve-step program for chocoholics? The Jerry Springer Show? How far? And then there's the matter of PMS…are we ready to face hormone hell sans chocolate? Be afraid, guys. Be very afraid.

In the meantime, it appears Moline has been blessed with an abundant chocolate supply. So I'll be there soon. Have chocolate, will travel. Or whatever…

—June 5, 1998 *The Dispatch*

SCENES FROM A DIVORCE

She walks quietly at my side, her small hand firmly in mine. She has a strong grip for her age. And determination.

She bathed and dressed herself this morning. Trying to help out. Trying to make a difficult day easier.

Overhead, dark clouds gather. Thunder rumbles in the distance. Dry lightning crackles across the horizon. The sultry air hangs thick, signaling yet another storm on its way. Both outside and in…

Inside, the courtroom is formal and quiet. Somber facial expressions reflect the serious climate. Others, like me, have come here to bury their dreams. It is not a happy place. Good things do not happen here.

We take our seats. Silently. No eye contact. It's best that way.

A minute passes. I hear my name called to testify. Yes, I'll tell the truth. And I do. My version of the truth.

Yes, we've tried everything possible. No, I do not contest any portion of the agreement. The details of the marital dissolution agreement are reviewed aloud. And then, the judge's final question: "Mrs. Ford, is there any hope—any hope whatsoever—of saving this marriage?"

I feel a penetrating stare from several rows behind. All mothers have invisible eyes in the back of their head. It's our best kept trade secret. It's how we always know what our offspring are up to. But on days like this, such knowledge is more a curse than blessing.

I will myself to look straight ahead. No eye contact, I remind myself. Do not look back at the past, this flat-lined marriage, or even her.

"No," I reply quietly. The plug has been pulled. "There is no hope." I glance down at my wristwatch. Time of marital death: 9:20 A.M.

An eternity passes. At least a minute. Maybe two. And then it's over. Case Number 98-140 Ford v. Ford is finally closed. After a record six-year separation, we are now officially divorced. Paroled from limbo.

During our separation, countless marriages began, ended, and restarted with new partners. Students began and ended college careers. Obtained degrees. And lived real lives.

Relatives died. Friends moved away. The White House weathered scandals of grand proportion. Wars were fought and won (or lost) in several third world countries. The stock market topped 10,000. And, one little girl grew from a baby into a third-grader wondering God knows what about the institution of marriage and the imperfect people given authority over her life.

It was a long, but necessary goodbye. And now it's hello to the season of uncertainty. The beginning of a journey without an exact destination.

In the car, she asks to play her favorite *Evita* tape. Staring out the car window, she sings along with Madonna's rendition of *Don't Cry For Me Argentina.*

She doesn't want to talk about this day. But I do. I need for her to know that this does not have to be her destiny. The cycle can be broken. And it starts with me.

Once upon a time, I was her. Thirty-five years ago, I made the same trip with my mother into a courthouse. When we emerged, life was never the same. And now, it's come full circle. I've become my mother. And another generation grows up without a father. The statistics of sorrow. For now.

I tell her that I believe strongly in marriage. Family. A home and hug to come home to. Every day. Forever.

She hears the words, but the sentiment is lost to the strained lyrics of a dictator's dying wife. "Where am I going to now?" laments the cancer-ravaged Evita. "Don't ask," replies her heartbroken husband. Even they could not keep their dream alive.

Later, in the quiet of late night, she sleeps peacefully. Another baby tooth is loose. Her tiny arms are still dotted with bruises from overzealous gymnastics on the swing set. Her hair is damp with the sweet smell of childhood. Her green eyes are closed, dreaming of tigers and pandas, toys and adventures, and whatever else dances through the head of a seven-year-old girl.

She looks the same as any other night. Almost. But something important was taken from her today. Something that can never be restored. Innocence.

Still, I have hope. Lots of big dreams. And a fervent belief in second chances.

In the meantime, Happy Father's Day to all dads, present or absent. Living or deceased. Myth or man. You are your children's best hope for a happy ending. And you are never forgotten. For better or worse.

—June 21, 1998 The Dispatch

HAPPY MOTHER'S DAY TO ALL
WHO GO IT ALONE

Today, millions of women will be rightfully recognized and honored for their induction into the great sorority of motherhood.

All of us who have ever done a tour of duty in the baby stroller brigade look forward to this day: Breakfast in bed. A bauble or two from a thoughtful spouse. Butterfly kisses. Fresh flowers. Homemade creations crafted by little hands using lots of paper and paste. Hallmark moments.

Large or small, fancy or frugal, the "stuff" we receive for Mother's Day reminds us that we matter. That the self-sacrifice that defines our every waking moment does not go unnoticed.

Then comes Monday. And back to what passes for normal.

Sadly, however, many mothers will go largely ignored today. Single mothers. Battered mothers. Elderly mothers who have had the misfortune to outlive their children. Estranged mothers who have grown distant from their children. Their—our—stories matter, too.

I am a third generation single mother. An early death claimed my grandfather. Divorce and an early death claimed my father. Divorce claimed my daughter's father. Never a break.

Today, I will be treating myself to something I can't afford. Something extravagant. Preferably in 14K gold. Or maybe gourmet chocolate. Godiva. Or even a babe outfit. Just to remind me there is life beyond estrogen. And the fact that no doting husband will be lavishing praise upon my chronically tired ears. My girlfriends got that life. I did not. Maybe next year...

In the meantime, I will console myself with the knowledge that my daughter's arrival in my life was the single best thing that ever happened to me. Whether or not anyone recognizes it.

Nova, now eight, is a new, better version of me. She will make a difference in the world. All of our children will. For better or worse. Which ultimately depends mostly on us. Scary.

Being a mother of worth is a job defined by constant self-sacrifice. From the moment someone places that tiny bundle of huge responsibility in our arms, we forever lose the right to put our needs first. For the rest of our lives, we will view every aspect of life through the lens of motherhood. And make our decisions—and sacrifices—accordingly.

Life was simple B.C. (before children). Live and let live. What others did was their business. Their walk didn't affect mine. So I thought.

For the last nine years, my daughter—and her welfare—are very much my business. Translation: everybody's walk now intersects either directly or indirectly with my maternal path.

Drugs. Drinking. Sex. Television. Music. The risqué advertisements in *Newsweek* (could someone please tell me why it takes a full-page ad featuring a naked woman to sell a computer?). The scandal that mesmerized a nation for a year. Columbine High School. Self-indulgent adults posing as parents. Self-esteem. Body image. Hot button topics. Cool trends. The list is endless.

The job is endless. And for single moms, it is done in solitude. Imagine making every decision for another human being single-handedly. No guidebook. No consultation. No crystal ball. No second chances. Very little forgiveness.

Some decisions appear minor and insignificant. Until twenty years later, when Johnny's doing time. Or Susie's in a twelve-step program. And then you wonder…

Others, huge and life-altering, can have dire consequences. Still others, unknown outcomes. Like my decision four years ago to homeschool Nova.

I will never know the outcome of Nova attending conventional school. Only the homeschooled version. Same with a million other choices we make for our children. Every hour of every day. Alone.

Imagine being bone tired by noon. Up to the wee hours of the morning with a sick child. Certain that you can't go on, but knowing you must. Living one paycheck from a homeless shelter. One dream away from the life you still hope to get. One universe away from security. Financial or emotional. One mistake from disaster. And so it goes. Being a mother is not a job. Or even a career. It is a lifestyle. It is forever. And too often, it is done alone.

So, to all the single moms: Happy Mother's Day. It is an honor to be one of you.   —May 9, 1999 *The Dispatch*

THE GOOD SHEPHERD

And so it begins. A new year and bad news arriving the same day. The tragic death of someone I knew a long time ago. Someone with whom I shared a birthday and a breathing problem.

Chuck Trapkus. The quintessential good boy. Always obedient to his parents. Respectful to his teachers. And polite to his peers. Totally uncool.

He was not the kind of kid that endeared himself to the ruthless rogues of the playground. Brute strength, not asthmatic underdogs rule. So, as a child, he spent a lot of time alone. But he never complained.

As an adolescent, he was, to coin a phrase, too good to be true. Never gave his parents, now long deceased, a moment of grief. To be honest, he was rather annoying. Parents (including mine) used him as the standard upon which to measure the insurrections of their rebellious teens. And we always fell way short of St. Chuckie. It was infuriating.

As an adult, Chuck became a controversial character who generated a lot of negative publicity over his radical beliefs. Whether it was his anti-war activism (usually in the form of a sit-in at the Arsenal) or his outspoken advocacy for the homeless, Chuck was the perennial fly in the social ointment. He "just got so upset over things *not* done to help the poor and homeless of the community," recalls Millie Buckrop, a longtime neighbor and family friend. "He had very strong convictions, and he lived by his convictions."

Just living what they taught us at St. Mary's. We are most definitely our brother's keeper, the nuns reminded us daily. Social justice was a moral imperative. To do anything less would be, well, Republican. And so *not* holy. Totally unacceptable.

Chuck was one year behind me at St. Mary's. An altar boy who once dreamed of becoming a priest. Of helping people less fortunate. Of doing the right thing. Always doing the right thing. It was in his blood. And embedded in his Catholic conscience.

When his mother, Mary, died from colon cancer in the mid-Seventies, Chuck was devastated. A few years later, his father, Charlie, also died from cancer, leaving Chuck and his sisters, Linda and Louise to stumble into young adulthood without the anchoring protection of parents. Luckily, all three eventually found their way.

In the early Eighties, while a student at St. Ambrose, I met a young woman with great faith and conviction. We attended the same weekly prayer group—faithwise, I was lost and Kim was found. So, we had little in common, except we were both in love. And, like all twenty-somethings, in the midst of great romantic turmoil. I was surprised to learn the object of her affection was none other than Chuck Trapkus. The good boy and the good girl. It seemed a match made in heaven.

But life had other plans. Although Kim and Chuck married, and eventually had two sons, Isaac and Paul, they divorced.

One day, years later, Chuck called on his old neighbor, Millie. He was looking for his roots—something to give his boys, he told her. Could she help? "He wanted his sons to know about their grandparents—things that he might not remember, from a child's perspective." So he brought them over to her house and they spent a good while reminiscing. "He was a really good father," Millie remembers.

A good son. A good brother. A good father. A good friend to so many otherwise friendless people. He lived the life he dreamed of—a life of commitment and conviction. An austere, frugal existence grounded in a sincere belief that we have a serious moral obligation to watch over the poor and downtrodden.

And that's how I will always remember Chuck Trapkus— a good boy who grew up to be a good man who tried his best to do his best. A good shepherd that always watched over his flock. And now, may the angels watch over him.

—January 5, 2001 *The Dispatch*

MISTRESS IN A BOTTLE

We're only as sick as our secrets. It's my friend Kevin's favorite aphorism to explain how the disease of alcoholism survives—and even thrives—in a culture that pretends not to notice the glaring inconsistencies between the rhetoric and reality of drinking.

Before plunging further into a volatile cocktail of trouble, let me say three things up front. First, I earned most of my way through college by serving alcohol at various bars and nightclubs. So admittedly, I've played a role in keeping people chemically content.

Second, I rarely drink. Never have. No desire. Brain cells are precious to me—none to spare. Thus, no incentive to wipe out a few million neurons in a single sitting. But I have known plenty of drinkers. Intimately.

Third, I struggle with two addictions. Chocolate. And shopping. My drugs of choice. So I understand, first hand, the mechanism of addiction. And I am far from smug.

Chocolate. Chardonnay. Cocaine. All the same. At least when it comes to brain chemistry. The same area of the brain lights up like a Christmas tree when any drug is introduced into the blood stream. Pleasure of grand proportion. Later, pain of grander proportion. What goes up must come down. But now is all that matters. Ask any addict.

Back to the secrets. Collectively, it is our best-kept secret: we are a nation of junkies. And we're really sick.

Nowhere is this more apparent than in our hypocritical on-going affair with alcohol (*aka* the drug that isn't).

Having a party? It won't be complete without booze. Taking a plane trip? Can't pass up those cute little bottles in first-class. Getting married? Don't forget the champagne. Holiday coming up? St. Patrick's Day practically mandates the flow of green beer.

Depressed? Need to take the edge off? Got a raise? Feeling good? Up. Down. Doesn't matter. Have a drink.

Drink to think. To avoid thinking. To flirt. Go to sleep. Wake up. To feel complete.

Where would we be without our mistress in a bottle? Sure, she's demanding. She lies. She's pricey. And, in the case of alcoholism, she eventually consumes everything around her. But she's also the great escape. Temporary freedom from chronic despair. A moment's respite from the demons. Anxiety reduction in a bottle. A best friend. And worst enemy.

As a society, we support this covert conspiracy in numerous (and seemingly benign) ways. Hosting dinner/birthday/Christmas/work (fill-in-the blank any excuse) parties that routinely feature alcohol as the guest-of-honor? Serving drinks before, with and after lunch? Consider sobriety and fun mutually exclusive?

Pouring booze for a spouse/friend/co-worker that has a drinking problem—and God forbid, letting them drive afterward, is dealing death. To the drunk. And to their victims on the road. Over 17,000 last year alone.

Covering for a spouse/parent/child when they're "three sheets to the wind" is called enabling and it's a problem, too. For both of you. Can we say, "co-dependent?" Enablers eventually become as addicted to the drunk as the alcoholic is to the bottle. So goes the dance of mutual destruction. That's why alcoholism is a family disease—it makes everyone sick. So if you're not part of the solution, you're part of the sickness.

Losing sleep over someone's drinking? Cruising the bars in search of an errant lover or spouse? Hoping to rescue him? Catch her in the act? Have a confrontation? Draw the line? Review all the broken promises in public? Hoping love will triumph? It won't. The siren song of the bottle came before you and will outlast you. To think otherwise is to engage in the most dangerous form of alcoholic thinking: denial.

Got a loved one with a drinking problem? These three things are true: you didn't cause it, you can't control it, and you'll never cure it. So, reach out to people that can help you. Al-Anon, a recovery program for families and friends of alcoholics, is a good place to start. There's one in every community. And it might just save your sanity. The alcoholic won't. Remember, we're only as sick as our secrets.

Alcohol is deeply embedded in our culture and likely here to stay. For example, *Newsweek* recently reported that alcohol advertisers spend more than $1 billion a year peddling their product—three times the annual budget of the National Institute on Alcohol Abuse and Alcoholism. Meanwhile, 14 million Americans abuse alcohol regularly. And countless others have to live—and die with the consequences of false advertising. How sick is *that*?

—March 4, 2001 *The Dispatch*

HAVE HOME, WILL TRAVEL

I just want to go home. I admit it. I own it (unlike the property I rent). And I live with it. Every waking moment—and even in my recurring dreams as I sleep.

This particular obsession to own began where most significant moments in my life occur—at the Dairy Queen counter. Let me qualify this culinary transgression to my purist readers… Whitey's does not exist on the road, and on the road is where I usually find myself. Always in the state of Perpetual Motion. Just ahead of the pain…or driving straight toward it. And in the middle…Dairy Queen. An inexpensive escape.

The pre-pubescent boy holds my Mocha Cappucino-Oreo-½ chocolate-½ vanilla Blizzard hostage. Not only has my special order required him to do actual math, it's forced him to do the unthinkable—seek adult assistance—and for that, he is supremely irritated. "That's $2.15," he snaps, still gripping my 'fix' in his hands.

I have two dollars prepared, but the change requires searching my purse (*aka* the black hole). Some pennies, a wayward lipstick, two rocks (Nova using my purse as central dumping again), a dime, and then…I stare down at the piece of metal in my hand…a tarnished brass house key. The key to my painful past, displaced present, and uncertain future.

A key that opens no door anymore. A key without a lock. An answer without a question. It is a key to nowhere. And a key to everywhere I've been.

It was at that moment I realized two things: One, I am homeless. And two, I want to go home. Desperately.

When my mother sold our family home two years ago, there was no time to react. The sale happened literally overnight. One minute my mother was an elderly, but independent homeowner living in the same house in Moline as she had for nearly fifty years, and the next, I was booking her a one-way flight to Nashville to begin her new life as a renter (separate column entirely).

In truth, "overnight" had been a long time coming. I just hadn't wanted to face it. That April, mom had become ill and been emergency-placed in a nursing home for thirty days. In May, after nearly three years on a waiting list, I got a call from the manager of a local elderly low-rise complex that there was a unit available for my mom.

In June, mom's next door neighbor offered to buy our house for her elderly mother. And then, on July 20th—the 25th anniversary of my father's untimely death—another unimaginable loss.

The house I was raised in—the house that always kept me coming back North, the house that was my only north in the constantly changing direction of my life—the only real home I'd ever known—all 660 square feet of it—now belonged to somebody else.

And now the key surfaces unexpectedly. A stark reminder that at age 42, I am in fact and symbol, homeless. A perennial renter. A rootless nomad. Fundamentally disconnected. And it's not just about real estate.

There is a still a house at 1844-32nd Street, Moline. But there is no home for me. Only memories. And now, this key.

Memories of sitting on the front steps waiting for my dad to pull up in his dark green Ford. Every Friday night and Sunday afternoon for eight years. Like clockwork. Until one stifling hot Saturday in July, when fate had a different plan—a massive heart attack at 51. So, he did not come the next day, as promised. But I sat and waited. And I'd go back to the front steps and sit—five, ten, twenty years later, and wonder…

There was a certain comfort in sitting on those steps…and lingering hope that maybe, just maybe I'd see his car turn off 23rd Avenue and head down 32nd Street if I waited long enough. And then my universe would resume normal tilt again.

Distant memories of outrunning the rambunctious neighborhood boys (one of whom is now a middle-aged homeowner in that very neighborhood), shoveling snow (cursing Illinois winters, vowing to one day move way South) and trick-or-treating in a safe, quiet neighborhood where elderly people always had a kind word and homemade treat to offer outline the seasons of my life.

The romances…the rogues…the family that never was, but always kept trying. These are my memories. And my key…

"That's $2.15," the boy repeats impatiently as the past, present and future collide in my already cluttered head. Currency for calories. Keys for keepsakes. It's a reasonable exchange.

"Another suitcase in my hand...where am I going to now?" laments the beleaguered Evita after another failed romance leaves her homeless and wandering the streets of Buenos Aires. I can relate. Do they have Dairy Queen in Argentina?

—April 5, 2001 *The Dispatch*

REMEMBERING THE SPIRIT OF '76

It's that time of life again. Another class reunion. The perennial yardstick by which we measure our ability to survive and succeed in the larger classroom of life. A grand opportunity for paybacks. Vindication. Absolution. And justice á la impressive titles and triumphs. It's the stuff of psychoanalysis—and the main reason shrinks take off the entire month of August.

Existential ironies reign at class reunions. Straight "A" students aspired to lives defined by "B's": boardrooms, babes, the Beltway. Jocks ended up living in subdivisions selling life insurance in places like Waterloo and Odessa. Former cheerleaders, now divorced from the former jocks, sell cosmetics at Neiman-Marcus (no, the ability to color-coordinate your eyeshadow with your sweater was not the most marketable skill to acquire in high school).

The most outspoken became a newspaper columnist. And I'm not referring to my colleague and classmate, John Marx.

The most creatively-challenged became politicians and newspaper editors. Random error and accident do not guide the universe, after all.

Our five-year reunion was characterized by a great deal of uncertainty and ambivalence. Who am I? Will I make it in the real world? Does my future involve French fries? These were the defining questions of the day.

Still, we viewed the world through the lens of individual immunity. Of course we'd make it. And we'd make it big. The world would bend to fit our needs, as the old song goes. The illusion of uniqueness remained intact.

Our ten-year reunion was a dress rehearsal for the part of bonafide grown-up. Marriage. Divorce. Offspring. A mishap or two. Maybe…just maybe, those tickets weren't stamped exempt. A small crack in the illusion created a vague sense of fallibility.

Our fifteen-year reunion was a wake-up call to those still entertaining the notion of personal exemption. Mishaps had evolved into tragedies. Untimely death had reared its ugly head and claimed spouses, infants, and peers. A new sense of urgency defined the day.

Change appeared imminent. Nothing would stay the same. We were heading into uncertain futures…ready or not.

Our twenty-year reunion featured fully-formed adults. The defining question was no longer "Who Am I?" We knew who we were. Worse, we knew who we weren't. And would never be. We were no longer led by illusions and fueled by fantasy. More days were behind than ahead…or at least more memories had piled up than ever before.

And now another five years have passed. A quarter of a century since the best and brightest went out to conquer a world already saturated with the best and brightest. As it turns out, the world did not bend, and even the prom queen learned a painful truth: most careers don't require a crown.

The invisible ones—those who drifted silently by through the years, learned an even more painful truth: real life is high school squared. Those days when cliques and cafeteria seating arrangements defined our existence are only a subdivision away.

However, there are some truths about my classmates at Alleman that will always transcend time and distance. Karen Gemignani will always be taller and blonder than me (although, thanks to heels and highlights, I can now hold my own). Since my maiden name was Gillespie, it was my lot in life to always stand in line behind Karen. For twelve long years (we also attended St. Mary's together). Lunch, recess, the bus stop. Always behind Karen. I'm probably still behind her somehow.

Lynn Lambrecht will always have flawless teeth and a perfect 300-watt Hollywood smile (her father was a dentist). Cathy Roberts will always look—and act like a classy movie star. Marlene Sleiter will always be our class celebrity, her "fifteen minutes" eternally airbrushed across the pages of *Playboy*. Mark Parkinson will always be grateful for the "A" I helped him salvage in Sister Judith Terese's Sociology class. And I will always be the familiar stranger they spent four years with.

The odd girl who preferred writing stories to dating. The invisible girl who worked in the cafeteria during lunch hour to pay her tuition to a school that was way beyond the means of a single parent. The intense girl who wore a black armband in protest of the Vietnam War. The outspoken teen feminist who, in 1973, wrote a controversial paper defending the brand new Roe V. Wade decision. A world away, nine men had decided that women now had choices. Easy for them to say. They did not have to spend the next three years in a Catholic high school. If we want your opinion, the Pope will give it to you, thank you.

Things are different now. Time is both a great equalizer and relentless predator. The truth is less black and white. More gray. With larger truths competing with the rules that were instilled in us. For example, it was easy to be pro-choice before I was actually facing the choices…and the consequences of those choices.

We've all faced many tough choices through the years…and soon, we'll assemble to reflect upon those choices. And recall with a sense of nostalgia, those days when our entire lives were in front of us.

Dreams still to be lived. Doubts to be conquered. And death to be defied. We were invincible. And now, we are what remains of the Spirit of '76.

—July 26, 2001 *The Dispatch*

SCANDAL SERMON SHATTERS SANCTUARY

Sunday. The one day around this house that remains sacred. No misguided mail announcing (or reminding) us of various familial and financial problems. No frenetic schedules to honor. No demons allowed. Just peace and quiet. In church, with my family, where all's quiet on the midlife front.

"Today, I have been asked to read a letter from our bishop," begins the deacon (aka lay minister, for my non-Catholic readers). An uneasy silence sweeps over the congregation. A collective, but silent groan. We know all too well what's coming.

The parish pastor settles into his chair at the opposite end of the altar as the deacon begins reading a lengthy and somewhat condescending (okay, kids, Father knows best...) letter explaining the recent sex scandal that has rocked the Catholic church to its exclusionary boy's club roots.

The letter also adamantly denies any cover-up (paging Bill Clinton) on the part of the church leadership regarding a local priest who is one of those charged with molesting young boys, and concludes by chastising the media (if we want your opinion, we'll give it to you) for their "misrepresentation" of the truth. Let the blame game begin.

My husband, a non-Catholic, and novice believer (bad timing to convert one's spouse amidst a scandal of Biblical proportion) whispers something in my ear about men trying to walk on water and paying the price. Acerbic remarks. I am squirming.

My 11-year-old Catholic-to-the-bone daughter, bored with the letter, has opened her Bible (ironically, a Protestant version) and found solace in Scripture. She knows some bad things are going on in our church. But her faith remains unshaken, insulated by the innocence of youth.

Looking around at the troubled faces staring at the pulpit, I feel totally demoralized. When did our church congregation become the studio audience for this week's bad episode of "Jerry Springer" (who coincidentally is in town this week working on his new album. Seriously.)? How did we come to this? More importantly, how do we move past it? Can we move past it? Or have we basically institutionalized insufferableness?

We Catholics are a somewhat arrogant, elitist bunch, often accused (rightly) of believing that our religion is the light, truth, and only way, which leads to the "higher you go, the further you fall" scenario now unfolding—unraveling—from Rome to Rio.

Non-Catholics (read: outsiders) think the answers to our problems are pragmatic: allow women to become priests and allow priests to marry. Which will happen three days after pigs fly and birth control pills are passed out with Sunday bulletins after Mass. The man in Rome will not even consider talking about it, much less thinking about it. Case closed.

Although I'm a cradle-Catholic, the answers elude me. On many core issues, I deeply disagree with Rome. Yet I come, week after week, year after year, with my family in tow because, like so many others, I need a sanctuary from the suffering and sadness of everyday life. A place where forgiveness can be given. A place that helps us face the uncertainty of tomorrow with a quiet heart.

And to be honest, I have only good memories of priests. Father Thomas Kelly sprinkled baptismal water on me as a baby, and many years later, while working at St. Mary's rectory, I sprinkled soothing eye drops into his cataract-clouded eyes. In 1972, Father Leo Gildner hired me to do clerical work for him and the other priests at St. Mary's. I was 13, and it was my first job. My earnings paid my tuition to Alleman High School.

While a student at Alleman, Father Daniel Mirabelli bought my textbooks and school supplies. Father John Lane gave me birthday and Christmas cards with fifty dollar checks enclosed. Why? Because I always saved him the biggest piece of cake on the lunch line (my second job to earn the remainder of my tuition was working in the school cafeteria).

At St. Ambrose College, Father Tom Stratman was one of my favorite professors. We disagreed about a lot, but he was always fair and open-minded.

As an adult, I've been blessed with the friendship of a truly amazing priest named Joseph Patrick Breen. An Irishman (obviously) with an incredible sense of both humor and the human condition, Father Joe Pat, as he's affectionately known, is the pastor of

St. Edward Catholic Church in Nashville. His compassionate and compelling homilies are the main reason our church is consistently packed to the rafters with non-Catholics as well as thinking Catholics.

All are welcome at the *Cheers* church, "where everybody knows your name and they're always glad you came." It remains a 300-watt beacon of light and goodness that continues to shine brightly through the darkness of despair that currently grips the Catholic church.

So we'll keep coming back. "As for me and my house, we will serve the Lord." (Joshua 24:15). Case closed.

—June 8, 2002 *The Dispatch*

ABSENT OR PRESENT—FATHERS MAKE A DIFFERENCE

My dad was no Ward Cleaver. He had his flaws. Namely women—he was married and divorced several times. And then there was the matter of me, born between two marriages.

When he died suddenly in 1974, at the age of 51, I was devastated. There was no grief counseling, hand-holding, or Prozac in those days. Not even a shred of empathy. What was the big fuss about, the neighbors wondered aloud. My father was, after all, just a "visitor" to my house. Not like a real dad who lives with his family and does all the heavy lifting of child-rearing (as if that guy existed in the sixties). And besides, since the child support ended with his death, and I was nearly sixteen, it was time to get a work permit and begin my tour of duty as family breadwinner. Priorities.

Thirty years later, you can still find me wandering through the rows of Father's Day cards at this time of year, reading the sentiments and reminiscing about the last Father's Day card I gave my dad. When he died two weeks later, I tucked it in the casket with him. He was also buried in the shirt I'd given him that Father's Day.

I can no longer imagine a life with my dad in it. Too much time has passed.

The first two decades were the hardest. There was always the problem of the "empty seat." High school graduation. College graduation. My wedding. Graduation, again (a poor factory worker's offspring earns a graduate degree). My daughter's Baptism.

Every milestone, every memory was tainted by the torture of the "empty seat." The place where dad would have sat, sharing my life as it unfolded if fate had not been so capricious.

I looked for him to appear at my high school graduation, telling me that reports of his death had been widely exaggerated. He was a practical joker—maybe he'd pulled the ultimate prank.

By the time my daughter was baptized two decades later, I had come to accept that death means forever. And forever means there will always be an empty seat in your world.

Still, just last month at my daughter's Confirmation (how quickly the third decade passed), there was a tearful moment when the Bishop called out her full name: November James Ford. My dad was there, through the granddaughter he never knew. A part of him lives on in her and her name. A small comfort embedded in a larger grief that never goes away completely.

In truth, I can barely remember the man who came faithfully every Friday and Sunday to "visit" me. The man who brought me books to read, scrap metal to build functioning telescopes with, and kites made of newspaper and cloth that flew high in the sky. The man who once chased off the neighborhood boys who were on the warpath over some perceived grievance against the only girl on the blue-collar block.

The man from Nashville who had a dream, not to make it in the music business, but to head North and find a steady factory job during the post-WWII years. The man who taught me the names of all eighty-eight constellations before I even knew my multiplication tables. The man who first showed me the brilliant rings of Saturn. The man who left too soon.

These are the scraps—pieces of memories so profoundly woven into the woman I've become—that form the DNA of my adult identity. And the reason my dad is still missed.

If he could show me the rings of Saturn at seven, what might he have taught me at seventeen? What would he have advised the confused 27-year-old bride?

What would he have told the overwhelmed single mother? Would he have been proud of his daughter, the college professor?

Would he have comforted the twice-divorced middle-aged woman? (I finally get it, dad—marriage is hard and people make mistakes. Sometimes more than one). Would he be sad for the daughter who still misses him and the traditional family that never was?

Despite the loss of my father, I have been blessed—I got to know my dad long enough to miss him. Many children are not as fortunate. Wars—distant and domestic—take thousands of men from their children every day. Other men, thinking fatherhood ends with conception, never show up. And some fathers alternately appear and disappear through the years, until they eventually fade from the scene altogether.

Their presence—and more profoundly, their absence—does not go unnoticed. Even three decades later.

—June 19, 2005 *The Huntsville Times*

LIVING LARGE IN DIXIE

In the interest of full disclosure, let me begin by saying that I am the exact average height (5'5") of women my age (fortysomething) and weigh 112 pounds. My almost 15-year-old daughter is one inch taller and weighs about the same. We are, in short, anomalies of the supersize era. And boy, do we hear about it. More on that later.

Last month, the Centers For Disease Control identified Tennessee as the fifth most obese state in the nation. Alabama fared worse—it ranked second in adult obesity (27.7%)—just behind Mississippi, which now holds the dubious distinction of being the leader of the pack in obesity rates. What's going on in Dixie?

Back in 1986, both Tennessee and Alabama had adult obesity rates of less than 10%. By 1987, both states had climbed into the 10-14% category and by 2002, obese adults made up more than 25% of Alabama's population. Tennessee is just a dress size behind.

Too many trips to Barnhills? Too many chili fries and Route 44 drinks at Sonic? Too much discretionary income in the nineties (maybe Clinton was a bad role model—Big Macs and a healthy economy—what was he thinking)? Too much time on our hands (before hurricanes and terrorism preoccupied our days)?

More important, what does it say about us as a nation when a full 65% of our adult population is overweight (30% of whom are morbidly obese—more than 100 pounds overweight)?

"It says there is an emerging trend that has to be dealt with," acknowledges Brian Williams, owner of Pride Care, a private ambulance service based in Nashville.

Thus far, Williams says he has invested more than $30,000 in special gear, including stretchers that can accommodate patients weighing up to 1,600 pounds, and a bariatric ambulance equipped with a winch and pulley system that can move the stretcher up and down a ramp "so the obese patient can be transported safely and with dignity." The equipment has also dramatically reduced back and leg injuries sustained by employees trying to lift patients who sometimes weigh 3-4 times more than average.

Is this a good thing? Or have we just psychologically resigned ourselves to exponentially expanding waistlines and innovative feats of engineering to transport and care for patients, who according to Williams, often weigh between 400-700 pounds?

Back to my daughter and me (now nibbling on a jumbo fudge chocolate chip M&M cookie while I write this) for a moment.

Over the years, we have both been subjected to unbelievably rude remarks ("does your daughter have anorexia?"), invasive questions about our eating habits ("you only eat *that* much?"), and rather bizarre observations ("you two are so thin—are you ill?") by our rather ample-sized peers.

Although I bite my lip and keep quiet, I always wonder how well it would go over if I, the thin person, reciprocated with an aghast, "You're eating *that* much?" Or, "you're really heavy—is it genetic or environmental?"

And, I think back to my twenties, when I struggled mightily with my own weight, once gaining over forty pounds in less than a year (too many midnight runs for bags of hot donuts and gallons of coffee ice cream). Not good when you're twenty-two and make your living serving drinks at an upscale club where the 'uniform' consists of shorts, a crop top, and heels.

So, like millions of other bingers, I had to finally face the dreaded 'D' word: diet (translation: Dare I Eat That—if it tastes good, the answer is invariably no). Ultimately, diet became a lifestyle of eating to live, not living to eat (as so many of us do).

It wasn't easy (ergo occasional cookie binges), but I eventually dropped the extra weight and felt so much better.

Being overweight is about way more than wardrobe limitations and double-wide ambulances—it's about deciding enough is enough and then transforming an 'all you can eat' mentality into a healthy respect for nutrition and fitness.

It's also about consequences—hypertension, Type 2 diabetes, strokes, colon cancer—and their cost to all of us. And it's about prevention— e.g., studies have consistently shown that watching television for sustained periods (sedentary activity while snacking on high calorie food advertised on television) is the number one predictor of childhood obesity.

But at least now we have ambulances and hospital equipment, including ceiling-mounted lifts and pulleys capable of moving patients weighing more than 1,000 pounds.

Is this a good thing?

—October 2, 2005 The Huntsville Times

BREAKING UP MEANS TOUGH CHOICES

My 15-year-old daughter recently learned a painful truth—she cannot physically be in two places at once. And, sadly, that is often what is expected from children of divorce.

Eight years ago, my daughter's father and I divorced amicably. There were no dramatic courtroom battles, custody disputes, shouting matches, or china flung across the room. Our marriage merely died a quiet death of indifference, and we went our separate ways.

Despite divorcing under the best of circumstances, there was one little complication—our daughter, Nova, who was then just 7-years-old. The best and most valuable treasure of our ten year union could reside with only one of us. For the other parent, she would be an occasional guest.

At the time of our divorce, we had been homeschooling for three years. I was Nova's principle 'teacher' and I was also self-employed. It made sense that she would live with me, solely. Her dad would visit when he could (he had accepted a job in a large city two hours away from where we were living) and life would continue pretty much as it had during our five-year separation (so cordial was our parting that we had lived together platonically since Nova's toddler and preschool days—my daughter and I in the upstairs of an older two-story rental home, her dad residing downstairs).

We honestly believed that divorce didn't have to hurt. At least not in the devastating way that sends kids to the couch for the rest of their tortured lives. We would be different. So we thought.

During the next few years, things did run pretty smoothly. In many respects, we were still a family—we just lived in different zip codes.

Birthdays and holidays were usually spent together. My ex-husband still mowed the grass and occasionally worked on our car when he stopped by to visit our daughter. And we'd all pile in his car and go out for ice cream afterward. The three of us got along great.

And then, three years after our perfect divorce, I remarried. Divorced. And remarried again. Each time, it seemed, there were new and unexpected problems. For example, my second husband, a divorced journalist, was stunned to learn that I expected our new 'family' to reside under the same roof, not in different states chasing down the latest great story. He disappeared from the scene quicker than you can say byline.

My last husband actually wanted us to all live together and even tried his best to make it work. We both did. But after five years, our midlife marriage finally collapsed under the weight of our collective baggage.

Remarriage, I've learned, is definitely not for amateurs. Or women like me looking for a family and a future. Remarriage is for the strong and confidant—and for those content to live in the moment. There is no shared past to bind your new 'family' together, no future that will not include people you never invited to the table. Nor even wanted at the table. There is only the present and that just isn't enough for sentimental types like me.

So, here we are, nearly a decade after our divorce, with me, the serial bride and divorcee (neither of which I am proud of), and my former husband, the one constant in both my daughter's and my life negotiating our biggest life change yet—his somewhat unexpected recent remarriage and all the trimmings that came with it, including a rather sizeable new family.

On the way to her father's wedding, Nova commented that she never imagined she'd be a bridesmaid in so many different weddings, all of them her parents. Then she dutifully donned her latest gown and took her place in line.

After the ceremony, pictures were snapped and my daughter joined a new family in progress. One that, as she would soon learn, required making difficult choices because now there were officially two entirely separate families that loved her, each wanting the pleasure of her company for birthdays, holidays, vacations, etc.

Yesterday, Nova's dad invited her to join him and his family for a Thanksgiving getaway. They'll be gone a week and as luck would have it, the holiday also falls during her sixteenth birthday. And so the painful lesson and true legacy of divorce—no amount of love, or even good will makes it possible to be in two places simultaneously.

For every yes, there must be a no, and when mom and dad no longer live in the same town, or even time zone, that means someone will inevitably miss certain holidays and milestones.

Realizing that difficult choices are part of doing business as a child of divorce, Nova recently announced her solution to these dilemmas—when she is an adult, she will celebrate every holiday at her house and simply invite us all. Whoever comes is welcome, whoever does not, makes that choice for him or herself. No more Solomonic choices for my child. Everyone is welcome in her life, regardless of marital status.

'SNOWHERE LIKE HOME

Several weeks ago, we had what's known here in the South as a "major weather event" which led the local news and required team coverage for several days. This "event" consisted of five inches of snow (isolated spots south of us received considerably more) with temperatures dropping…are you ready for this…into the low teens for several straight days. And we had strong winds, too.

The result of this meteorological calamity was total shutdown. The snow began falling late Sunday night which resulted in local schools closing preemptively. They did not reopen until Friday, and then parents were advised to "use discretion" about whether or not to send their children to school.

Business came to a halt, stores were shuttered closed, Kroger was a wasteland of empty shelves, and even Wal-Mart was a ghost town.

The three major interstates that straddle Nashville were littered with abandoned cars, police implored people to stay home, and streets went unplowed and unsalted (already dangerously low on salt, our county rationed out the last of its precious mineral on major arteries and on-ramps to I-24, leaving secondary streets untouched).

Dire predictions were made, including everyone's least favorite: children may have to attend school this summer because Metro-Nashville has already used up its ten allotted snow days (back in December we got three inches of snow, which resulted in another other week off).

You probably read about this "event" in the newspaper and perhaps laughed at the sight of major cities like Atlanta and Nashville brought to a standstill. That's why they lost the war, you figured.

And you're probably right. That kinder, gentler approach to both life and weather cost us the war.

But not the one we fought 150 years ago. That one was rigged. It's the other war that I'm concerned about. The one nobody talks about.

Those secret little battles we constantly fight with ourselves over whether to behave with character and class or to join the Jerry Springer crowd, whether to dialogue and debate issues with sublime integrity or shrill ignorance. If you've ever had a major weather event of your own, you have to decide whether to embrace it as an opportunity to be enjoyed (extra time at home with loved ones), or a crisis to be endured (extra time at home with loved ones).

Frankly, this latest epic snowstorm made me wax nostalgic for the good old days in the 'hood on 32nd Street when my next door neighbor, an imminently stubborn, but lovable Croatian woman named Virginia Churuvia, and I once trudged six blocks through waist deep snow to the old Geifman's Grocery Store in the King Plaza Shopping Center.

After congratulating ourselves for powering through Alberta clipper winds and bone-numbing cold, we quickly got down to business and judiciously loaded our cart with non-perishable food items. In the likely event of a power outage, our precious cargo would not spoil.

It was not until we were back outside, weighed down by heavy grocery bags of canned goods, that an unfortunate fact reared its ugly head. We had to walk back home, carrying eight sacks of canned goods between us. What were we thinking?

Expletives and a vow to one day move South, where I'd never have to shovel another flake of snow, followed.

And so I did.

But I never forgot our excellent adventure to Geifman's. After we cursed our lot in life, Virginia looked out across the snowdrifts that obscured the parking lot and said, with quiet resolution, "Well, the only thing to do is to do it."

And so we did. In stoic silence.

Thanks, Virginia. You taught me a powerful life lesson about the value of perseverance which has served me well through many seasons of life. Including major weather and life events.

Author's Note: On December 14, 2012, Virginia died at the age of 89.

PART TWO
LOVE WITHOUT BORDERS:
My Life as a Mom

DOUBLE X EQUALS DOUBLE STANDARD

A quiet, peaceful Sunday. That's all I wanted. No misguided Republican fan mail. No threatening phone calls from creditors. No deaths in the family. No impending romantic disasters. No worries about Nova. All quiet on the mid-life front. Tranquility would not elude me today. So I thought.

"Mom, I want to be a priest when I grow up," my daughter said matter-of-factly as she got in the car after Mass. "For real."

Excuuuuuse me? My daughter thrives on the outrageous. I accept this. I savor it. Like mother, like daughter. Still, there are times when even I crave conformity. Advantage apathy. Tranquility. Obviously, not today.

"You want to be a priest when you grow up," I repeated with the same flat affect exhibited by catatonic schizophrenics and Republican presidential candidates. Nine miles of bad road ahead. I did not want to go there today. But Nova did. "I love God and I just want to talk to people about God," she continued. Simple. Rational. Realistic. In another life. Another gender.

A quick mental inventory of standard replies left me in a rare moment of speechlessness. Supportive fell way short of the mark: Gee, honey, that's a terrific idea. Three days after pigs fly, the first woman priest is expected to be ordained. Encouraging a choice that doesn't exist smacks of deception. Discouraging her choice is a feminist faux pas.

Less thrilling was the prospect of defending the practice of institutionalized sex discrimination. Worse, I would then have to explain the annoying reality that haunts every female every day of her life: the double standard. It was the moral equivalent of admitting the Easter bunny is bogus.

Tranquility was not only eluding me, it was being annihilated by a five-year-old's declaration of career choice. Or, as I was now duty bound to explain, lack thereof.

I told Nova that the Church has a rule that says only boys can be priests. She did not look impressed. Her response: "How come girls can grow up to be presidents, but not priests?"

Well, my precious Double-X offspring, you probably can't be president, either. Not as long as the gender gap between rhetoric and reality continues to swell from the welts of the backlash. Just ask Hillary. Or any woman who has struggled for visibility in male dominated classrooms and careers. Ask any woman who has experienced the imbalance of power in everything from personal relationships to public policy.

Memo to guys: Is there any sense of accomplishment in constantly winning a race that's rigged? Just curious.

A slow descent into the grim estrogen pit where the monsters Oppression, Discrimination, and Victimization reside in misogynistic harmony had begun. Such an insidious process. First Santa Claus. Now this. I should have seen it coming months ago. Watching me cut out a newspaper photo of the Republican presidential candidates (keeping tabs on the opposition) Nova had asked, "How come there aren't any girls in the picture? Don't Republicans allow girls to be president?" Good questions.

She continued, "Is it because the only girls…well, women… that are Republicans are those guys' wives and of course they don't get to be in the picture?" Close. It's called protected status. That privilege has a price: personal freedom. And the right to be in the picture.

Today, my daughter's world is full of possibility. She wants to be a priest. She also wants to be a psychologist, artist, doctor, architect, and astronomer. Like most children, her interests vary. Unlike many older girls, she still believes she can be anything. Her self-esteem has not yet been eroded by years of struggle to achieve in a world largely designed, defined, and dictated by men. She has not yet watched her body grow while her options shrink. The double standard has not yet arrived to stake its claim. With one glaring exception, her career choices seem imminently attainable.

And what about that exception? Does it really take a Y chromosome to make a deposit of faith? Or is this just another "No Girls Allowed" sign posted at the entrance of a boy's club fearing invasion or—God forbid—improvement through inclusion of women to its growth stagnant ranks? Either way, my daughter has a simple solution: "When they build our new church, they should build new rules, too. That way I can be a priest when I grow up. And so could other girls."

Our church building is undergoing renovation because we have outgrown it. Maybe the rules could use some renovation, too. Let's face it. This is not your father's church any more. Ready or not, the girls are coming.

Equality may be a bitter pill to swallow, but it's nothing compared to choking down the jagged little pill of rebellion that defines the Alanis generation. *Caveat emptor*, guys.

—May 17, 1996 The National Catholic Reporter

WE'RE NOT IN KANSAS

Last summer, my daughter developed a sudden interest in Indians. As did 32 million other preschool scholars. The *Pocahontas* bug.

My response was simple. We'd go see real Indians. Experience real Native American culture. It was a given that we'd have one Kodak moment after another to cherish for the rest of our lives. Typical baby boomer overkill. My daughter would not be conned by the crass commercialization of history. A legacy cannot be licensed. Even by Mickey and Co.

Armed with my esoteric elitism, I began planning our itinerary to the nearest Indian reservation. Which, as it turns out, was only 900 miles away (I was on a teaching assignment in northwestern Illinois). Practically in the neighborhood, I sniffed. With the noblest of intentions, the field trip from hell had been conceived.

First, we went to the library and checked out every available book on South Dakota and Indians. Plains Indians. Indian customs. Folklore. And Indian wars. You name it, we read it.

Next came the planning stage. I painstakingly planned every detail, including stopovers at the Great Plains Zoo in Sioux Falls, the Corn Palace in Mitchell, and the Badlands National Park.

No detail was overlooked. I was obviously a perfect parent, mentor, and planner. The Peter Principle had silently claimed another victim.

The first day of our trip was spent traveling across Iowa. We did not see the famous bridges. We saw only cows and corn. My only distinct memory of Iowa is stopping in the tiny hamlet of—get this—Pocahontas, Iowa to ask for directions. I was shocked to see a human gas station attendant cleaning the windshield of the car in front of me. When he finished, I heard him say something I've never heard uttered at a gas station: "Thank you. Come back soon." Having no basis for comparison, I may be wrong, but I think he was sincere.

When he approached the car, I stiffened. Like a Pavlovian dog, I have been conditioned to expect the worst when a stranger approaches. Carjackings, not courtesy, define urban life.

I finally cracked the window and asked for directions. He patiently explained that I needed to go back to the landmark Pocahontas statue and turn right instead of left. In other words, do just the opposite of what I had done. His words would prove prophetic.

The second day of our trip was uneventful because the eastern half of South Dakota is uneventful.

At the Great Plains Zoo, I dutifully explained each animal's place in the great circle of life. Whatever Disney does, I can do better. Smug tends to be synonymous with stupidity.

After Nova fed the llamas, rode the pony, watched the primates play, and visited every form of animal life from penguins to pandas, she looked around and said, "Is this it?" Reality was beginning to rear its ugly head. I ignored it.

After a tour of the world famous Corn Palace, Nova said, "Well, I guess I'll have a bag of popcorn. Since all there is here is corn…"

I ignored my pint-sized vision of disillusionment and continued on.

We spent the third day driving across the rest of South Dakota. I found myself contemplating the sense of futility that must have engulfed the early settlers when they first arrived on the high prairie. No Dillard's. No gourmet coffee bars. No cell phones. The suicide rate must have been phenomenal.

Traveling on foot or even by covered wagon for weeks only to find yourself staring at endless jagged rock formations probably sent many a pioneer over the edge. Literally. But only after much self-recrimination. If only they'd turned the other way. Less bloodshed and better shopping. Another valuable history lesson.

The sight of an approaching mini-van broke my reverie with the past. Inside were a family of four. The flurry of activity among the passengers offered a brief respite from the monotony of the road. Exaggerated gesturing and tense facial expressions lent support to my theory: a shared gene pool doesn't always mean a shared reality. The driver, a fellow baby boomer, appeared mired in the throes of midlife angst. Had he found his salvation in South Dakota? From the looks of things, no. The wheat logo passed in a blur. Back to Kansas.

Of course, we're different, I convinced myself. Delusion had replaced denial.

On the fourth day, we arrived at our final destination. The Badlands. "Now," I announced triumphantly, "we'll see real Indians." And we did. At a Texaco outside Wall, South Dakota. Three Indians dressed in Levi's and plaid shirts stepped out of a Toyota Previa.

"Where are your feathers?" Nova asked dejectedly. "You're not real Indians." She continued, "My life is ruined. I want to go home."

Explaining that Hollywood distorts reality by producing and packaging an illusion means nothing when you're four. Neither does the concept "politically correct."

On the way home, I glanced in the rearview mirror and was horrified to see I bore an uncanny resemblance to the guy from Kansas. I looked at Nova. "Did you have *any* fun on this trip?" I hated being in parental purgatory.

"No," she said with finality. "All I wanted was to see Indians. My life is *still* ruined." Forgiveness was not to be mine.

This summer we're going to grandma's. It's cheaper. Besides, I need the money for therapy.

—July 29, 1996 *The Tennessee Register*

THE FACE OF HOMESCHOOL

When my cousin, Nina, announced that she was going to homeschool her children, no one in the family was particularly surprised. We live in the South. We have our standards here, including the widespread belief that whatever can be accomplished by an institution can be better accomplished by an individual. Didn't we once fight a war over this principle of individualism?

Most of us were impressed with Nina's initial enthusiasm and energy. Three years later, she still believes she chose the right path to educational enlightenment. Consistent enthusiasm is such a rare thing these days.

I became curious. Of course, *I* would never homeschool my child.

In fact, until my mainstream cousin came out of the educational closet, I always associated homeschool with religious fanaticism, hermits, cults, and other "fringe" types. Now I wondered what else I didn't know about homeschooling.

First, I learned that homeschooling is far from the province of the fringe. Rather, it is a growing trend in education among some of the most intellectually fashionable. For many parents I interviewed, homeschooling had been a two-thumbs down referendum on both the beleaguered public school system and its blatantly bourgeois alternative, private school.

Many parents have become disillusioned with the lockstep mentality that characterizes public education. A system that rewards conformity, penalizes innovation, and has built its very foundation on sustaining mediocrity does little to inspire confidence and respect.

Then there's private school. Maybe it's just sour grapes about not being in the overclass league, but for me, private school is not a realistic alternative.

Secondly, choosing to homeschool means choosing a lifestyle. It means thinking in a different key. It means a preference for divergence. It means making a commitment to actively participate in the world where our children live. Homeschool is about nature walks, live experiments, and field trips. For a kindergartener like my daughter, Nova, it also means building a bridge from verbal language to print literacy. It means discovering the beauty of dandelions in December, water color paints, and long forgotten songs promising mockingbirds and diamond rings to those who fall asleep without fussing. Homeschooling means facing incredible challenges and struggles. Ultimately, it requires the ability to surrender the promise of a final destination in exchange for the magic of 'right now.'

Third, homeschooling means answering the most bizarre questions. Some commonly asked questions (and responses guaranteed not to generate a follow-up interrogation) include:

Q: Does your child have a medical problem that prevents her (him) from attending regular school?

A: Yes, she's allergic to mediocrity. We both are. (A well-timed sneeze can add a nice touch of dramatic flair).

Q: Why would you undertake such a task?

A: Why *wouldn't* I?

Q: Can you financially afford to homeschool? (A favorite among mother-in-laws)

A: The gene pool is against me. I can't afford not to.

Q: Aren't you worried about "socialization?" (The trump question—if you get past this one, you're homeschool free)

A: (To those with children in private school): Have you looked around your child's classroom lately? Wake up and smell the Latte; it's a whiter shade of pale.

A: (To those with children in public school): Is that what they're calling crisis intervention these days?

Looking back, I'm not sure exactly when I began to reevaluate the radical idea of homeschool. I just always wanted to keep an open mind about my options. I interviewed parents, teachers, school psychologists, and, of course, kids. I read books on home education and reviewed the data. I studied the assessment scores of children who had been homeschooled vs. those who attended public/private school (overall, homeschoolers have significantly higher standardized scores in all subjects). I visited schools and reviewed a variety of curriculums. Finally, I did what most parents do in times of uncertainty—I went with my gut.

On the last day of summer vacation, we took a drive over to the school Nova would have attended. Since young children are known for their fickleness, I decided one last acid test of sincerity was in order. "Last chance for a normal education. What's it going to be?"

"Homeschool," she answered matter-of-factly, and then continued, "because I want to learn and you're the *bestest* teacher." Sappy, yes. But so pure in her belief that she can learn and I can teach. I knew we'd make a good team. And the stories we'll have...

—July-August, 1996 *Home Education Magazine*

FROM EMPATHY TO ALTRUISM:
COMMUNITY SERVICE

Of all the research on child development I have read, absorbed, lectured on, and applied to parenting, one particular topic continues to fascinate me: the development of empathy (or lack thereof) in young children.

Is there a gene for empathy? Some researchers say yes. A child is either a born empath or not. Sure, you can preach empathy, and engage in selfless, altruistic behavior, but if Johnny was born to be bad, it's going to be a constant uphill battle.

Other developmental theorists are convinced the environment plays the critical role. Plenty of nurturance, clear limits on behavior, and rewards for prosocial behavior facilitate the development of empathy. Parental modeling can also go a long way toward raising young altruists.

The old nature-nurture debate rages on. However, the findings of most studies on altruism (empathic behavior) suggest a combination of practicing and preaching empathy leads to an increase in altruistic behavior. For example, social psychologist David Rosenhan conducted a study on altruism among the children of civil rights activists and found children whose parents had been freedom riders in the Sixties exhibited more altruistic behavior than those whose parents had simply preached civil rights, but not acted in their conviction. Other studies have yielded similar results.

In my opinion, empathy is the hallmark feature of a civilized society. Without it, we are lost. Still, it took the birth of my daughter to force me to admit that my lofty rhetoric far surpassed the reality of my everyday experience. I always meant well. And sometimes, my empathic feelings did evolve into altruistic action. But more often than not, I was too busy. Too tired. Too lazy.

Then came my social conscience in the form of a child. From the moment Nova came into this world and staked her claim on my restless heart, I knew I would have to measure up. Under Nova's constant scrutiny, I have stretched myself past capacity. I don't seem any worse for the wear.

If there is a gene for empathy, Nova has it. As a toddler, Nova would sit patiently on my elderly mother's lap while I wheeled them for hours around the local mall. Every week for three years we repeated this ritual. Though confined to a wheelchair, my mother never had any discipline problems with Nova, either. Nova seemed somehow to sense my mother's physical limitations and responded accordingly. Cupboards were never locked. Gates never erected. Treasures were not put up.

By the time Nova was a preschooler, adults had learned to edit their speech—not so much for expletives, but emotional content. Nova's ability to pick up on subtle emotions and body language made for an attuned and formidable preschool presence. She asks difficult questions. And she's intense. Like mother, like daughter.

This year, Nova and I found a way to put our empathy to practical use by adding a community service component to our home-school curriculum.

Every Wednesday, we deliver Meals-On-Wheels to twenty homebound senior citizens in our small town community. Our route takes about three hours to complete and includes some of the most beautiful scenery in the rural South.

We have met elderly people from all walks of life and in various states of health. We've heard both tragic and happy stories. And we've learned some important life lessons, i.e., the worst case scenario is a combination of poor health, poverty, and old age. As a baby boomer, this seemingly obvious revelation has been a wake-up call. More years are behind me than ahead. A freelancer in outlook as well as occupation, I need to start planning for the future.

Nova has also learned the healing power of a hug. The joy of service to others. Most importantly, she is learning to actively participate in the world around her. To "show up" both physically and emotionally. Not from the distance and detachment of youth, but with the empathy of a fellow human being.

Nova has also acquired numerous practical skills as a result of her volunteer work: reading a street map and signs, learning directions, counting and sorting meals according to regular or diabetic diet, and memorizing the menu (she loves telling our clients what's in their lunch).

Alzheimer's Disease. Stroke. Hypertension. Rheumatism. The relationship between weather and chronic ailments. Old wives' tales. History. Story telling. Decline. Frailty, both physical and emotional. Nova is familiar with both the terms and the result.

She has experienced first-hand the restorative power of human contact. For instance, several of our clients wait by their doors, eager to see my daughter emerge from the car. They wait patiently, yet with a sense of urgency. Time is their most valuable commodity. They have precious little left. Nova knows this, too. We've talked about the possibility that each visit may be our last. Especially with our very elderly clients. Nova's reply is always the same, "of course, you could die, too, Mom. So could I. In my sleep…anywhere." She's right. Nobody has the promise of tomorrow.

So we go back, week after week to visit our new friends. We need them as much as they need us. Mutuality. That's what friendship is all about.

Nova just walked by and asked what I'm writing about. When I told her, she said, "tell them I really like those elderly people…and I'm really glad I know them. They care about me." Anything else? "I like their hugs…it's like I'm important to them."

That's what empathy is all about.

—January-February, 1997 *Home Education Magazine*

WHEN HOMESCHOOL ISN'T PARADISE

When I first began researching information about home-schooling, I received two excellent pieces of advice from veteran home educators. First, if you're going to homeschool, education has to be more than a job, or even a career. It has to be a lifestyle. Pure and simple. Secondly, if anyone can talk you into or out of homeschooling, it's not the right choice for you. Homeschooling requires an incredible investment of time, effort, and energy. Therefore, it has to be a calling from within. Deep within.

The first piece of advice was easy for me to affirm. I went from college to graduate school to teaching without missing a beat. Before the birth of my daughter, the classroom was the center of my universe. It always seemed to be the one place that made sense. The place where my restless mind could find peace. Either side of the desk was fine—the opportunity to debate current issues, exchange ideas, and meet truly interesting people was addictive.

When my daughter, Nova, was thirteen months old, I began teaching part-time in the Psychology department at the university where I'd received my graduate degree. Nova had become a regular fixture at the school since before birth (I became pregnant the last semester of grad school), so it seemed perfectly natural for her to accompany me to the classroom. Besides, I was teaching Child Psychology, and Nova provided a perfect audio-visual example of infant development. Then toddler development. And the following year, preschool development.

Both colleagues and students welcomed Nova. She had many adventures in the department's rat and pigeon lab, the assessment area, and of course, the classroom. For Nova, the university was a playground, the place where "mommy earns money for food and toys," and where fun people hang out. She also loved eating lunch at the campus cafeteria and perusing the nearby bookstore. Like mother, like daughter.

In the blink of an eye, my pint-sized assistant was old enough to start kindergarten. It was time to say goodbye to my students and leave the formal classroom to begin homeschooling the most important student I will ever teach.

The second piece of advice also seemed like a 'no-brainer'. My decision to homeschool was based on years of professional training and research. More importantly, the decision to homeschool Nova was based on personal conviction.

Every parent, regardless of professional training, is their child's chief advocate and mentor. Nobody knows a child's needs, fears, strengths, and weaknesses as intimately as his/her parent. Every parent is an expert where their own child is concerned. But, as I would soon learn, expertise and perfection are not the same.

I had read the research, studied the test scores of homeschoolers vs. those who attend public/private school (homeschoolers score consistently higher across all subject areas), visited schools, interviewed parents, children, and teachers, and studied various curriculums. The one thing I had overlooked was real life!

It would take many months (truthfully, the entire first year) of trial and error for me to get on track. There were many days I threatened to deliver Nova to the doorstep of public school and never look back.

I remember reading an article in a home education magazine about a family who began each day at 6:00 A.M. with bible study and a full breakfast cooked from scratch. By 7:00 A.M., the dad was off to the office, and the mom was busy homeschooling their four children. After reading the article, I felt totally defeated. I have rarely seen 6:00 A.M. unless I've stayed up all night. A pop tart and a glass of milk constitute breakfast in our house. And class begins at 9:00 A.M. (give or take). Still, we carry on because, in my heart, I believe homeschool is the right choice for us. But this year, I'm more realistic about the whole process. I've learned the hard way that homeschool, like childbirth, is a highly unique experience to everyone who does it. You can do all the reading and research you want, but until the water breaks and someone yells "push," it's just a spectator sport. And it's always easier said than actually done. Hopefully, the suggestions below will help ease some of the labor pains.

1. Don't compare yourself, your curriculum, or your teaching philosophy with anyone else's. As parents, we measure ourselves against impossible standards (e.g., the Cleavers) and then become

frustrated when we don't measure up. Perfect parenting is no competition against the relentlessness of daily life. Mortgages, marital difficulties, and worries about money usually win over the most noble attempts at perfection.

2. Know and accept your limitations. No parent is 100% knowledgeable 100% of the time. That's where tutors, other parents, friends, co-workers, and even the public school system can come in handy. For example, once a week, Nova attends a two-hour class for the gifted at our local elementary school. Her teacher is certified in special education and can offer Nova the benefit of her expertise. And since Nova is an only child, she gets the benefit of learning to work in a group of peers.

3. Field trips are your friend—use them! For younger children, sitting still 4-5 hours a day is torture. Field trips can provide an exciting and informative respite from the monotony of workbook activities. And they provide lasting memories of shared experiences. A cave, state park, historical site, museum, zoo, dairy farm, water treatment facility, planetarium, botanical garden, cheese factory, and a pizza-making demonstration were all part of last year's itinerary. Many sites offer reduced or free admission if you mention that your visit is a field trip. Also, home educators can go as a group and take advantage of group discounts.

4. Know your child's learning style and make it work for you. For example, when Nova was learning to read, she would get very frustrated with the phonics approach. I also got sick of speaking in monosyllables—repetitiously sounding out every single word was miserable for us both. I finally realized Nova is a whole language learner. She memorizes entire words and then uses illustrations and familiar words to provide cues and context.

5. Realize that no two children come assembled the same. What works successfully for the homeschool family down the street or in a magazine article may prove a total failure for me. And vice versa. Even siblings can be very dissimilar in learning style, temperament, and motivation—so just when you think you have it down pat...

6. If homeschool isn't working for you and/or your child, it's not a personal referendum on either of you. For me, the most difficult aspect of homeschooling has been financial. I know I will eventually have to return to paid teaching. Homeschooling from a

homeless shelter would be carrying my conviction to an extreme. Each year, I must balance my concern with the needs of my daughter. Again this year, I chose sacrifice over financial security. Next year, security may take precedence.

Occasionally, I think about the family in the magazine and wonder if their days are still as idyllic as portrayed in the article. Regardless, I'm happy with the life I got and the opportunity—even if it's only for a few years—to homeschool my daughter.

DEATH, TAXES, AND UNKNOWN OUTCOMES

Five months ago, most of America was playing armchair quarterback about whether 7-year-olds should fly airplanes. As usual, I was on a different page. Since I have trouble letting my daughter even cross the street alone, the kid-in-the-cockpit issue also seemed rather bizarre.

Actually, my first response to Jessica Dubroff's death was incredulity. I remember watching in awe as her mother faced the media and spoke coherently about Jessica's dream. Imagining myself in her place, I saw a future involving psychotropic medication. A vacant stare. A padded room. Far from camera-ready.

Truthfully, I did not feel a lot of maternal kinship. Besides, my attention was focused elsewhere.

While the rest of America was agonizing over death and taxes, I had a less benign adversary to face: the public school system. A multi-disciplinary team (M-team) consisting of a classroom teacher, special education teacher, principal, school psychologist, and me were meeting to determine whether my daughter could enter first grade in the fall. The problem was not academic. Nor was it emotional, social, or maturational. It was her birthday.

Five-year-olds, by definition of state law, are not eligible to attend kindergarten if their birthday has the misfortune of falling on the wrong side of an arbitrary cut-off date. Nova's birthday is in November, well past the September 30 deadline. However, two years ago, Nova was tested and certified intellectually gifted. This does not mean she is certified a superior human being. In fact, giftedness is a mixed blessing/curse. Nova's life will not be easy. Already, she can outreason, outmaneuver, and outwit most adults. On some level, that has to be scary when you're five. Power is such a fickle companion. It can turn on you so quickly. And somehow, we will both have to find a way to live with that reality.

One way is early entry into school. Forcing a child, who by age four had mastered all the basic skills of kindergarten, to wait until she is almost six to receive any structured form of education is worse than negligent. It is patently absurd. Studies have found that gifted kids who are held back until age mates catch up tend to wash out academically by third grade. For a 5-year-old, a steady diet of boredom is toxic.

The other members of the M-team did not agree. Their decision to make Nova repeat kindergarten (I homeschooled her for kindergarten, assuming the age cut-off would no longer apply for first grade) wasn't really a surprise. Rarely are educators accused of innovative thinking. Nor are they particularly fond of studies involving hard data that support opposing views.

Educators do, however, love to tell "war stories." For example, the kindergarten teacher justified her veto by explaining that her now 15-year-old son entered kindergarten early and it had been a disaster. Seems he's totally traumatized by the fact that he's the only one in his class not old enough to get a driver's license. His current sullen mood is a direct result of early admission into kindergarten. Excuse me, aren't all adolescents sullen? Blaming adolescent angst on early school admission was a new angle. Similar to blaming homeschool for Jessica Dubroff's death. *Homeschool Proves Fatal.* I still expect someone to propose a connection.

The school psychologist explained her veto with this dire prediction: If Nova goes to first grade, she will likely succumb to peer pressure in junior high. Drugs. Alcohol. Promiscuity. The usual sundry evils. "Hi, I'm Nova. I'm an alcoholic because I started kindergarten early." Give me a break. Did she understand the concept of individual temperament and its influence on behavior? It's pretty simple. Traits such as shyness, influenceability, need for achievement, self-confidence, etc. are a function of individual temperament, not chronological age. Thus, the oldest kid in the class can also be the most immature. Conversely, the youngest is sometimes the class leader.

Finally, the trump card: socialization. Okay, conceded the gang of four, maybe Nova can make it academically, but can she cut it socially? I explained that she attended a kindergarten Sunday School class every week. And a physical education class twice a month with other homeschoolers. That she could go from playing with age mates to sitting quietly in my college classroom with ease by age three. They just didn't get it. Lockstep mentality prevailed.

While five adults were voting on her future, Nova had been down the hall, sitting in on a regular kindergarten class. After the meeting, I had watched from the doorway while she interacted with peers she'd just met. Friendly. Confident. Normal looking. I did not have premonitions of her face, concealed behind sunglasses and a hooded sweatshirt, adorning a future post office wall.

When I explained the M-team's decision to make her repeat kindergarten, Nova's first response was: "Have I failed?" Absolutely not. "The system failed," I replied. "So, homeschool, grade one, begins this fall." We will not worship at the altar of conformity. Instead, we pray for the best and then go our own way.

Push. Hold back. Parenting is a constant balancing act. Whether it's early entry into kindergarten or the cockpit, there are no easy answers. No crystal ball to show us how a different decision would have played out. No second chances. No guarantee of a favorable outcome. Sometimes dreams become reality. And other times, they become the genesis of a eulogy.

By the end of that early spring day, solidarity had cast its long shadow from a small town in California to a small town in Tennessee. Children have a way of doing that.

Note: Our second year of homeschool began August 19th. Nova and I continue to enjoy the discovery process involved in homeschooling.

—October 3, 1996 *The Dispatch*

LOVE WITHOUT BORDERS

"*For where your treasure is, there your heart will be also.*" Matthew 6:21.

Another Valentine's Day and here I sit doing something very unusual. Nothing. No romantic disaster of the week to survive. No obsessive ruminating about the lack of happy endings for aging Cinderellas. No Clintonesque dramas unfolding in fact or fiction. No stalkers pretending to be suitors. No slick quips about the misery—er, men in my life. No emotional autopsies waiting to be performed. All's quiet on the estrogen front. Too quiet...

So, before beginning my annual Valentine ritual of gouging out the undersides of every piece of gourmet chocolate (I still hate surprises—I like to know what I'm getting before biting into it) in the heart-shaped box calling to me from across the room, I want to tell you a story about true love—love without borders. Without boundaries. Baggage. Or breakups...

Just a little over ten years ago, my daughter, Nova James (named after my long-deceased father and his love of astronomy) arrived to stake her claim on the restless heart of an aging Cinderella who had seen and done it all. Gouged out all life's surprises from the inside out—good and bad. There were no surprises left. So I thought.

There is always one surprise left. The faithful call them miracles. Cynics defer to the theory of random error and accident. I prefer to believe that for once in my chronically distressed life, when Nova showed up, the angels prevailed.

Although she's growing up under the vigilant eye of a neurotic mother who obsesses over her every thought, move, and deed--and then writes prolifically about it—Nova rarely complains.

Strangers read about her most embarrassing moments and private matters. Everything from her first words to toilet training to her secret prepubescent longing for an Elmo doll (she just walked by and glancing at the computer screen, remarked with great horror, "You're writing about that again—now everybody will know.") has appeared in print.

From divorce to death to depression. From Barbies to bad boy behavior to the Beltway. From our quirky homeschool odyssey (six years and counting) to losing our home. Whatever the topic, Nova has consistently been my best source. But more importantly, she's my best friend. I more than love her—I actually trust her. And for some inexplicable reason, she believes in me, too. More than I deserve.

She even endures (with minimal groaning), the ultimate horror of pre-adolescence: wearing matching mother-daughter outfits. Black jeans. Leopard-print tops. And leather hikers. Way cool stuff. Especially for a size two mom reliving her youth.

Ours is a once-in-a-lifetime relationship without borders or boundaries. Although much of it has been preserved on paper. And in all my best memories.

Life as it's being lived. Love as I've never known it before. And joy as I've never experienced it. I am so glad she showed up just when she did.

In retrospect, I had been waiting all my life for her to show up— I just didn't know it. Wandering around geographically and emotionally gets old after a while. Lost and lonely grows tedious—especially when you get past thirty. But to find my way home, to find that special place of the heart that only a child can lead the way to, I first had to find her.

Nova gives me direction. A dream to follow. And plenty of forgiveness. She is both my anchor and my flight of fancy.

She is a newer, better version of me. She's all the things I might have been if circumstances—namely life—hadn't intervened.

She stands by me when the rest of the world turns its back. She brings me homemade Valentines—the paste and paper kind, lovingly constructed by little hands that have yet to be held by someone that will break her heart. She is still innocent. And for that, I am supremely thankful.

She reads me bedtime stories—like I read her years ago—to comfort me on nights when the demons linger and lightness is long gone.

She is the embodiment of hope—and the main reason I stick around. I want to see how this show unfolds. And, to be honest, I want to have at least a cameo role in the drama of her adult life.

She is my treasure. And my heart is with her. Today and always.

Happy Valentine's Day, sweetie. May you always get the piece of chocolate you most want. And may we always have plenty of everything we need—each other.

—February 14, 2001 *The Dispatch*

A Day In The Life Of A Single Mom

Yesterday, my ten-year-old daughter, Nova asked, "Why is there a special day for moms, dads, and grandparents, but not us kids…don't we deserve a break, too?" Yes, my precious offspring, you most certainly do deserve a break and you got one: *me*.

Remember last Tuesday? The day from mommy hell…

It started shortly before midnight Monday when you announced that you couldn't sleep. Seems you had a sore throat. And I had thirty research papers still to grade.

After twenty minutes of comforting words and a dose of children's Tylenol, I walked you back to bed, promising your sore throat would feel better by morning.

I continued grading papers until nearly 2:00 A.M. At my age and that hour, words start blurring together, so I took a mental break, imagining my girlfriends safely tucked into their comfy beds with their princely husbands (2 A.M. is my hour of self-pity), bills all paid, and lives on track. Unlike certain single moms. Slitting my wrists held renewed appeal. Until I saw you appear in the doorway, looking quite pitiful.

Silently, I took your little hand in mine, and we walked down the hallway to your bedroom. I tucked you in and sang, "Hush Little Baby." You drifted off to sleep. And then I went to bed for my "nap." The alarm was set for 7:30 A.M. so you could leave at 8:00 A.M. on a field trip.

Since you were already dressed and seated at the kitchen table working on your social studies assignment when I dragged myself out of bed five hours later, I was encouraged. Your throat was still sore, but you really wanted to go on the field trip.

You looked pale, but admittedly, maternal concern was slightly overshadowed by the looming fear of not having a lecture prepared for my class. I needed those three hours.

Your ride arrived at 8:00 A.M. promptly. We hugged goodbye. You felt a little warm, but…the lecture…the papers…the insanity of it all…

"She's burning up, dizzy, and really sick…" explained my friend Joyce from her cell phone a little over an hour later.

"I got here as fast as I could," reported my friend as she emerged from her car shortly after the ominous phone call. "And by the way, Nova threw up twice on the way here."

I reached into the backseat and picked you up. Fortunately, you weigh only sixty pounds. Unfortunately, I weigh only 105.

My lecture on happiness (biting irony) was done. I've learned to speed read and memorize with frightening accuracy my "lines" for any given class. But now came the question of what to do with you. I couldn't cancel class—it was the last session before final exam week. More papers were due.

I couldn't leave you home alone for the afternoon. Your dad was on a plane to Denver. My elderly mother shouldn't be exposed to a virus. And other moms are great—until it involves a sick child.

So, I fed you some soup, and off we went to school. As we've done so many times through the years.

I asked a colleague if you could rest in his office, but he had to leave immediately to pick up his kids from school. He offered to let you ride along, but when I told him you had a fever, he quickly re-considered.

My secretary had taken the day off. Her office was locked tight. So, you sat quietly in the back corner of my classroom with your head down, looking quite ill. And me feeling quite guilty. Single Mom Syndrome (S.M.S.).

I delivered my talk on happiness (note: the psychologist who did the pioneering research on happiness eventually committed sui-cide—either because he learned there is no such thing as happiness or he was a single parent) dressed in black, head to toe. Dramatic flair. My forte.

After class, I raced home, dropped you off to rest, and then headed to Kroger for ginger ale, the mini pizzas you were craving, more medicine, and a thermometer.

The day before, I had returned a pair of shoes I'd bought re-cently. Tightening up the budget. The refund was $17.33. Your food craving and medicine came to $17.24. Single moms never get ahead. It's a fundamental law of the universe.

After dinner, I set your plate on the counter, intending to wrap up the food you didn't eat. Then, I reached for a glass in the cupboard above. It slipped. And suddenly, glass shattered across the counter and your plate of leftovers.

After cleaning up the mess, I checked your temperature again. 100.6°. Another dose of acetaminophen, a bedtime story and snuggle. And finally, lights out. It was now 10 P.M....twenty-two hours after you first complained of a sore throat.

The next morning *I* had a sore throat...

You asked why there's a special day for moms? Many Tuesdays, my child. Seven days a week. Three hundred sixty-five days a year. For a lifetime.

Now I have a question for you, my darling daughter: Where's *my* present?

—May 13, 2001 *The Dispatch*

HOME AWAY FROM HOME EDUCATION

Every Monday morning three determined women, 107 home-school students from Rutherford, Bedford, Coffee, and Franklin counties, a dozen-plus teachers, and one shared dream of educational excellence converge at a rented church building in Murfreesboro. The result is an oasis of organic learning and discovery geared specifically toward the needs of homeschoolers, grades 7-12. An 'unschool' amidst a plethora of public and pricey private schools. And, for one day a week, a home away from home.

In 1999, Barb Daniels of Winchester, Diane Cothern of Murfreesboro, and Cathy Leftwich of Gladeville (a small community near Lebanon) found they had a shared problem. Each had tried to enroll their child in a Nashville tutorial but found them all closed. The number of area homeschoolers had risen so sharply that all the tutorials were full.

In Rutherford County alone, 330 families representing nearly 1200 homeschool students belong to Home Educators Are Rutherford's Treasures (H.E.A.R.T.), the area's largest home education association. "And that doesn't count all the families who have joined other, smaller associations," says Mark Lee, Co-Director of H.E.A.R.T.

Concerned they would not be able to provide adequate coursework for their 7th through 12th grade students, the three veteran home educators began discussing ways in which to start a new tutorial that would serve Rutherford and adjoining counties. With nine children and over four decades of combined homeschool experience between them, it wasn't long before the 'founding mothers' officially opened the doors to the Rutherford Tutorial Academy (RTA).

Thirty-four students enrolled the first year. Enrollment doubled the second year and has continued to grow steadily ever since. Currently, 107 students attend RTA, which according to Daniels, is "right about where we want to keep it." A wide array of classes are offered, including a full complement of Math (e.g., Algebra, Geometry, Trig), Science (e.g., Biology, Chemistry, Physics), Social Studies (e.g., American and World History, Economics, Geography), English (e.g., Grammar and Composition, American and British Literature, Speech) and Foreign Language (e.g., Spanish, French, Latin) courses. Other course offerings include Computer Science, Drama, Accounting, and Philosophy.

Small class sizes offer an intimate and highly focused learning environment for the serious student. "There is a maximum of twelve students per class," says Daniels, "with an average class size around ten students."

Tweens and Teens begin arriving at the church building a little after 8:00 A.M., and then disperse into various classrooms for courses that last a little over an hour each. Study hall is available and required for students with breaks during the day. The last class lets out at 4:30 P.M. There is no cafeteria, so students have the option of either bringing a sack lunch, leaving the 'campus' with their parents, or relying on Leftwich to provide pizza and soda for a small fee. "Every Monday, I order seventeen pizzas," says Leftwich, adding, "the kids get two pieces of pizza and a Coke for three dollars."

Although there is a definite Christian slant behind the RTA philosophy, the founding mothers purposely chose to avoid doctrinal emphasis. "We wanted a place where all faiths could come and feel comfortable," explains Daniels, adding, "We even use some public school curriculum." Including science materials that present a balanced view of both creationism and evolution, the latter theory notoriously unpopular (and therefore often arbitrarily avoided) with many Christian homeschoolers.

The teachers, or tutors as they're more accurately known (RTA is "not a school," points out Daniels, "rather, the parents remain their child's primary 'teacher' while tutors provide expertise in specific areas the parent may not feel qualified to teach"), have varied backgrounds. Most come equipped with Bachelor's, if not Master's degrees. Some, like English tutor Valerie Brandon of Manchester, are certified teachers as well as home educators themselves. Math/Computer Science tutor Tony Buchanan, also from Manchester, is a retired engineer. Others, like Drama tutor Tina Hutchison (former singer and current Drama Director at First Baptist Church, Smyrna) and Spanish tutor Miriam Redmond, a native of Cuba, and veteran home educator, bring years of life experience as well as a thorough knowledge base to the academy.

"We recruit tutors by word of mouth," explains Daniels of the academy's somewhat unorthodox approach to hiring faculty. "We put the word out, and they come to us." Somehow, it all seems to work—well enough that new classes are added yearly.

With enrollment at RTA approaching capacity-level and no plans to expand, other tutorials are now springing up throughout Rutherford County to meet the growing needs of middle and elementary-age homeschoolers. For example, Legacy Tutorial in Smyrna serves sixth through eighth grade homeschoolers, and Junto (named after Benjamin Franklin's circle of intellectual friends) Co-Op serves students in grades K-8.

Back at RTA, the weekly classes will keep going as long as the students keep coming. But what will happen when the 'founding mothers' are no longer homeschooling? "We haven't really discussed it," says Leftwich casually. "We'll figure something out." Translation: they'll pray on it. "Absolutely," smiles Leftwich. And of course, there's word-of-mouth. The tutors came to them, and so will the future administrators.

In the meantime, these women are on a clear mission. "We want our kids to figure out who they are before everyone else tells them who they should be," explains Daniels of the RTA philosophy. Cothern, the mother of three children, all homeschooled from the beginning, concurs. "My oldest son (Jeremy, a junior at the University of the South) recently told me that for him, one of the big advantages of homeschool was not having other kids constantly telling him who he should be, how he should think, how he should dress." Still, she readily admits that homeschool is not for everyone. "It takes up a lot of time, and you have to be completely focused."

And, so it goes on the educational road less traveled. A delicate balance of laser-lock focus and frenetic energy. Sustained commitment to an unusual lifestyle. Lots of prayer. And a genuine belief that home is where the school should be. Except on Mondays, when RTA becomes home for a day.—October 19, 2003 *The Tullahoma News* / —December 28, 2003 *The Daily News Journal*

NOVA'S FAITH JOURNEY

Parents of teenagers worry about a lot of things. Namely the four deadly D's—dating, drinking, driving, and drugs.

Even peripheral thoughts about malevolent threats to the health and well-being of our children rob us of sleep, serenity, and eventually, sanity. And that's before they're even born.

If we're supremely lucky, childhood passes without incident. Then, one ordinary afternoon, amidst the chaos of happy meals and homeschool, cartoons and cellular phones, and preferring cool to cute, adolescence arrives. And with it, not one of the four "D" words, but an announcement from my cradle Catholic daughter.

"I've decided that in my heart, I'm a Baptist, not a Catholic. I've also decided to officially join the Baptist church."

My child's quiet certitude renders me speechless.

Nova has been thinking about becoming a Baptist off and on for nearly two years. Almost constantly for the past few months, she adds. "I still feel emotionally at home in our church because we have so many good friends there, but at the Baptist church I feel spiritually at home—closer to God." And isn't feeling spiritually at home more important, Nova wants to know. "I mean friends are great for now, but God is forever." Case closed.

Compelling wisdom from a 12-year-old. Too compelling to ignore.

Suddenly, anticipatory dread fills the air. Through the years, I had mentally prepared for eventual confrontations about dating and peer pressure, not articulate arguments by a savvy adolescent who has decided she's trapped in the wrong dogma.

To arbitrarily dismiss Nova's religious declaration as a 'stage', put my parental foot down, and veto any further association with the Baptist church (she had been attending services as a guest of our neighbors) might be the easiest course, but I know my child. She has not arrived at this spiritual crossroads without considerable thought and prayerful reflection. Therefore, I owe her at least one sleepless night to ponder this unexpected turn of events. But, I warn her, "I am far from ready to deliver you to the door of another faith just yet."

After several intense discussions with my husband (a non-Catholic civilian), our pastor, the Baptist pastor ("I can't believe I'm here—but it seems my daughter believes she is one of you..."), and Nova's godparents (one Catholic, the other, Baptist) about this spiritual 'detour,' I am more confused than ever.

The consensus—let her go. For now, at least. Otherwise, she might grow disheartened and lose faith altogether.

Letting go is for those with the luxury of detachment, not for parents. So, I finally decide, we will all go—on a 'sabbatical' of sorts—to see where God leads us.

Thus begins an unexpected journey. A family adventure down a spiritual road *way* less traveled. With no promise that we'll ever return home together.

The itinerary is simple. We will attend the Baptist Church every Sunday for six months. During that time, we'll also attend Saturday evening Mass. Nova could work at the Baptist Church (she applied for a teacher's aide position during their upcoming vacation bible school—seeing her sport a Baptist 'staff' tee shirt a few weeks later was a bit jarring), but she must also work at our church's VBS.

We would read a book on the Baptist faith together and meet with both our pastor and the Baptist minister to explain our journey. But if any one of us wants out of this pilgrimage, we'll stop. To do what, I don't know.

"So, what do y'all think?" Nova asks as we struggle through the sea of well-dressed people exiting the mega-sanctuary of her new church 'home' three Sundays into our journey.

"Bombastic. Theatrical. Too many pyrotechnics," observes my husband, the cynic. "But they have a great sound system." Deafening drum kits, not dogma impresses the family musician.

Nova looks crestfallen and turns to me. My assessment is worse. I can tolerate the somewhat manic service. And as a writer, I can even appreciate the use of multi-media (guest speakers appear on big screen televisions suspended midair throughout the auditorium) to keep the huge audience, er, congregation riveted to their seats.

The occasional, "Amen, brother" uttered by congregants to underscore agreement with the pastor's forceful sermon is a bit distracting. But it is the frenetic free-floating exuberance exuded by every person that we have contact with that leaves me spiritually shell-shocked.

"We are so excited to have you with us." "Just thrilled you could join us," gushes one stranger after another. Others, sporting radiant smiles the width of Texas, are "honored," "blessed," and deliriously happy that three Catholics have apparently seen the light.

"God has a special plan for Nova—He's working through her for a great purpose," beams another ecstatic congregant.

Never having seen a Catholic thrilled, or even noticeably enthusiastic when someone visits our church, I am unsettled by such abundant energy.

Catholics are not an excitable bunch. We are a reverent, introspective, guilty group. And that's just the way I like it. My religion matches my personality.

Another six weeks pass in a blur. Our journey has become a slog. My husband audibly groans when the sermon on tithing concludes with an invitation for the congregation to enroll in the church's new electronic transfer of funds option—sign-up cards are passed around and it's business as usual.

My breaking point comes the following Sunday, during the early days of the war with Iraq. Listening to the car radio on the way to church, we learn about the heavy fighting in An-Nasiriyah. At least 10 Marines have been killed already that morning. Somebody's children would not be coming home alive. Every parent's worst fear.

Sadness defines the day. And the urgent need to be somewhere quiet where I can pray. And think.

The upbeat, contemporary Baptist service seems even louder than usual. And more removed from reality. The drums bang and the crowd power praises. No mention is made of the carnage unfolding half a world away.

Chronic bliss in the face of death and despair. Charming but somewhat vacuous. And definitely not me.

Having reached my saturation point, I leave midway through the service and head across town to kneel and say a rosary for the dead soldiers. My husband, still glazed over from the direct deposit debacle, dutifully follows. Nova stays behind. Her friends will bring her home later.

In her heart, Nova still believes she is meant to be a Baptist. And no amount of cajoling, bargaining, or reasoning convinces her otherwise. We are a family divided and drained.

"This never would have happened if you hadn't let her visit that church to begin with," remarks one parent after Mass when another inquires about Nova. "I never let my kids visit other churches. It just confuses them."

Mentioning that Nova's paternal grandparents are Baptist, or that every summer since she was three, we've visited various churches so we can learn about how others worship is pointless. Nova's faith journey has evolved into a referendum on parenting styles, not a time of spiritual insight.

More days pass. More prayer. And more angst.

If I force Catholicism on Nova and she loses faith altogether, what have I accomplished? On the other hand, God had given me authority over her, and maybe He expects me to make the choice for her.

It is a conundrum I cannot resolve. Nova is in God's hands. Whatever His plan for her, so be it. If she is meant to be a Baptist, then my hope is that she'll be the best Baptist ever. If she is meant to be a Catholic, then God will help her find her way home.

Just three days later the phone rings and a stranger tells me that Nova has been hurt at the Baptist church. Something about a door, an injured finger, and a lot of blood.

Turns out, a heavy wood door had unexpectedly swung closed, trapping Nova's index finger in its hinge. One of the adult chaperones (it was youth group night), a nurse, had bandaged it, but clearly, the injury would necessitate a trip to the emergency room.

Later that night, after her broken finger is numb and stitched up, my daughter holds up her bandaged hand and quips, "Well, that's it for me—I got the message—this is God's way of telling me to come back to the Catholic Church."

On the surface, it sounds rather flip, but in truth, Nova had been secretly praying about her faith journey and essentially come to the conclusion that although she likes the Baptist church a lot, deep down, she is really a Catholic, after all. She just needed a sign from God to confirm what she already knew.

So it's true that God never closes one door without opening another. Literally. But the larger truth is that Nova's faith journey helped all of us grow as individuals and as a family. It was an unexpected, but necessary trip.

—March 4, 2005 The Huntsville Times

MCLEARNING: I TEST,
THEREFORE I AM

Every year, my daughter and millions of cohorts sit in class-rooms across the nation, pencils in hand and standardized test booklets, *aka* their future, spread out before their glazed over eyes.

For my daughter, testing is a minor aggravation, a hoop she must jump through to be eligible for scholarship money. She tests well—actually very well. I say that not as a statement of maternal pride, but as a caveat to other parents of 'gifted' children. Watch what you wish for. The testing treadmill is relentless and unforgiving.

First certified 'intellectually gifted' in preschool, Nova was simp-ly a kid who loved to learn. Everything from vocabulary words to complex sentences. Simple addition to asking really sophisticated questions—and then retaining the essay answers I eagerly provided. Devising creative solutions for problems. All of these were pre-'I test, therefore I am' (burned out) Nova.

Fast forward ten years. The heat is on. College tuition is be-coming increasingly out of reach for many parents (e.g., the Ten-nessee Board of Regents recently approved a 9.7% hike in tuition at state colleges and universities—the third in as many years). Private colleges have long been prohibitively expensive and homeschool college is not yet an option.

Competition is stiff and the stakes are unbelievably high as I learned when academic advisement became part of my job descrip-tion as visiting lecturer at a small liberal arts university in Iowa back in the mid-nineties.

Distraught students would arrive like clockwork at my office just before Christmas break (reality rearing its ugly head through a string of unredeemable grades) seeking Solomonic advice about their un-fortunate predicament.

Glancing at their dismal grades and hearing desperation in their voices as they teetered dangerously close to academic failure often begged the question, "What brought you here to begin with?" Nothing in their grades, demeanor, or tear-stained faces suggested any real passion for the demands of college. So, what had brought them to this place?

From their many stories, a disturbing picture of well-intentioned parental pressure combined with sheer terror emerged. It had been ingrained in them, almost from birth, that there were two ways to go in life—college or a career in fast food. There was nothing in between. A life in the corner office or a life at the drive-up window. It was all up to them—and their test scores.

So they had taken one test after another until they reached the magic score that opened the door to the university. The problem was, once through the door, they were required to think. And since testing does not equal critical thinking, the performance problems began almost immediately.

Of course I dared not tell them that acing a standardized test did not mean they possessed the real skills necessary to succeed in college, e.g., the need to achieve, perseverance, self-discipline. It simply meant they tested well. And with enough practice, anyone can test well (it's called *practice effects*), including marginal students who spend their entire tour of duty from kindergarten through high school blackening circles with a No. 2 pencil.

But not to worry—it appears a new day has dawned in higher education. Adapting the K-12 'Test Until You Drop Model', many colleges no longer require thinking. For example, I recently turned down an offer to teach at a community college after hearing that I wouldn't need to generate a syllabus, select a textbook, or I suspect, even think.

"We already have a master syllabus and textbook," the Dean explained, "so that every student on every one of our campuses is taught the exact same course material and therefore performs consistently well on outcome tests." McLearning. Wow—now there is a third choice in life—fast food mentality in a classroom setting. My former students would be pleased.

For my daughter, homeschooled, but tested yearly in the public school system (cynic that I am, I still recognize the weight assessment carries), the footrace is on. She must score well on the ACT to graduate a year early; extremely well to be eligible for serious scholarship money. Additionally, she must successfully pass the Gateway Exams (Tennessee state requirement) in Language Arts, Biology, and Algebra, and she will have to manage a stellar performance on the SAT to hopefully win a coveted seat in a college classroom where thinking is still required—if she can even remember how to think after having the joy of learning tested out of her.

—July 31, 2005 The Huntsville Times

REFLECTIONS FROM THE FINISH LINE

"So, what's it going to be," I asked my four-year-old daughter. "Me or a normal education?"

It was August, 1995 and the two of us were sitting in the parking lot of the nearby elementary school where my daughter, Nova, was scheduled to begin her tenure as a student that fall.

"Homeschool," replied a confident voice from the back seat. I looked back at the angelic face of my one and only. I wasn't so sure. My life was so chaotic—her father and I had separated, my part-time job as a college instructor was about to end unless I agreed to go full-time and I had an elderly mother in poor health. Little did I know those would later be fondly remembered as the 'good old days.'

Sensing my hesitation, or maybe because she was simply wise beyond her years, Nova smiled sweetly and repeated, "Home-school," adding, "Because I really want to learn and you're the *bestest* teacher ever."

How could any sane, rational 36-year-old adult say no to that smiling face, so sincere in her belief that we'd make a good team—me the teacher, she the quintessential learner. Sappy? Sure. But the stories we'd have…

And the stories we lived…

Thirteen years, three states, six relocations, a midlife career change, three marriages (her dad and I did divorce and eventually remarried others), taking care of a now very elderly and incapacitated mother, and over three hundred field trips to everywhere from the routine (police station, bread factory, zoo) to the exotic (the Northwest Trek, the Viking trail in Newfoundland, a Dragon Museum) to the esoteric (operas, musicals, stage plays, lectures by creative intellectuals) later, we are wrapping up the final days of our long and complicated homeschool journey.

A dozen years ago, a veteran homeschool mom offered me some sage advice that I have often passed along to the next generation of wannabe home educators: Homeschooling is not a job. It is not even a career. It is nothing short of a lifestyle. So if you're ready to adapt a lifestyle, best of luck. If not, walk away."

As one of the few who continued homeschooling through the high school years (aware of the high stakes, many parents understandably quit homeschooling after eighth grade), I would add: this is no trip for amateurs.

Homeschooling in the early years is mostly about fun, friendship, and field trips. High school, on the other hand, is all business. The business of both running a school competently and being knowledgeable in multiple disciplines, including math, science, language, the fine arts, and social studies (high school teachers are usually certified in just one or two areas of study). Having a special talent (say, film production), skill (marathon runner) or interest (quantum physics) is especially helpful in designing interesting electives for your student.

Finally, homeschooling throughout high school means playing the role of empathetic guidance counselor (transcripts, financial aid forms, scheduling college preview days, academic advisement, and setting up ACT tests, etc., are all your personal responsibility as is your child's performance on said tests because you're the one who either prepares them adequately for the demands of college or permanently ruins their chances of adult success). Home educators do not have the luxury of blaming Mrs. Smith's lack of teaching experience or Mr. Jones' bias against their child when academic setbacks or even failures occur (and they will, even for the best and brightest learners—e.g., my daughter initially struggled mightily with Algebra I, but two years and much self-discipline later, mastered Geometry with minimal effort).

All the administrative duties that go along with running a school (because that's what you are—an independent, private school that receives zero funding from any sources other than your own pocketbook, which is usually empty) including curriculum planning and development, field trip management, course electives, and record-keeping are also the sole responsibility of the parent.

Most of all, homeschooling means going against everything society says matters. For example, last spring, I accompanied my daughter to a nearby university where I saw a former colleague of mine across the room— a freshly minted PhD when we last saw one another at a teaching conference—being introduced to the visiting high school students as Chairman of the school's Psychology Department.

Seeing a junior colleague who once suggested I try for a tenured position at the private school where he taught was a bit jarring, especially since he is both much younger than me and now running said department while I am basically unemployed.

For the first time since beginning this odyssey, I wondered whether I'd committed career suicide. Will I ever work again? For anything above minimum wage? My skills are so twentieth century…unless you count my uncanny ability to win, hypothetically, large sums of game show money (yes, I am smarter than a fifth grader because I have repeated all thirteen grades as an adult, thank you).

If really understanding why Andrew Jackson became our seventh President, pondering the obscure principles of institutionalized poverty, and debating the finer points of the human genome project counted for anything monetarily, I'd be rich. But, as it stands, I'm just a well-read has been. On the other hand, my daughter is a very well-read (perfect 36 on the Reading subtest of the ACT—and I do take full credit for that), well-adjusted (unlike the fringe kids the media always finds to personify homeschool, Nova mingles well with all age groups), and gracious (hand writes thank-you notes) young adult who has never given anyone a day of grief (well, there was seventh grade which was pretty miserable for us both, but then all tweens are miserable).

So, would I do it all again? Of course—if it were August, 1995 and that same four-year-old gave the same sales pitch. Because it turns out she was right—we made a great team. And the stories we have…

—March 9, 2008 *The Huntsville Times*
—September, 2008 *Nashville Parent Magazine*

PART THREE
CONFESSIONS OF A RENEGADE YANKEE
IRISH-CATHOLIC DEMOCRAT

THE RAW DEAL

Several months ago, I received a call from a reporter at *USA To-day*. To a struggling freelance writer, such a call is analogous to a starving actor receiving the message, "Hollywood called." My head was spinning. Which of my essays were going to be published? My dream of having a syndicated column was beginning to look less delusional and more visionary. I mentally resigned from my "day" job of teaching. My ink pen, ideas, and initiative were going national. One of my prolific essays had finally caught the eye of an enlightened editor.

A moment later, my flight of fancy crashed and burned when the voice at the other end of the line said, "We're doing a series on the needs and concerns of the elderly and I'd like to get a few comments from you." I was thirty-six. What did I know about being elderly? I teach a course in Lifespan Psychology and frankly, when we get to the section on late life development, I wing it. I am scared beyond words of the aging process. I also realize that as individuals and as a nation, we are doing pathetically little to improve the quality of life for the eldest members of our collective family. Still, I did know enough to say yes when asked to be a part of the Tennessee Democratic Party's Task Force on Senior Adults. I may lack the experiential aspect of older age, but I am genuinely concerned about the needs of the people who helped raise me—my mother, former teachers, and neighbors. I needed them to help me grow up and now they're counting on my generation to help them face an uncertain future.

I answered the reporter's questions. We talked mostly about the practical needs of the elderly. Safety issues, specifically, fear of being victimized by crime appears to be a big ticket item among senior adults (as it is for most of us). The precarious state of Social Security and Medicare also rate high on their worry list. For example, my mother subsists (not to be mistaken for "exists") on a meager Social Security check that lags far behind inflation. At 74, she continues to work part-time to supplement her stipend from Uncle Sam. The deductible and co-payment portion of her Medicare make anything short of lifesaving medical treatment impossible. The poor (many of whom are elderly women) continue to experience the wrath of Ron and Co. that characterized a twelve-year reign of terror in Washington.

As another election year approaches, we're faced with some difficult decisions. Do we continue to support the legacy of altruism that began with The New Deal? Or do we adopt The Raw Deal advocated by many Republicans, and just say no to the needs of the elderly poor? Does my generation continue underwriting the costs for our weakest links? Or, should we dismiss them with a cavalier "let them eat cake" mentality as we cruise down the information superhighway toward the 21st century? Taking care of the elderly, the poor, and the disenfranchised is so low tech. And we're such a high tech generation. Look at our responses thus far. We've created elaborate databases and generated complicated statistics in a feeble attempt to quantify human misery. We study, measure, and analyze the needs of the elderly from the distance and disinterest of youth. Then we make public policy based on computations rather than compassion. Baby boomers are the ultimate problem solvers. And problem makers. Just ask our kids. They've had to live with the legacy of our detachment.

Fortunately, a few of us still care. We may not know the exact solutions, but we do know that the problems facing our parents and grandparents are real. The future is now, and ready or not, we have to face it with integrity. The eyes of our children are on us. The decisions our children make tomorrow about our care will be determined by how we shape policy today. We're all in this together.

—January 15, 1996 *The Tennessee Register*

HILLARY'S NOT-SO-EXCELLENT ADVENTURE ON THE HILL

Remember those pesky little boys in the third grade who were constantly trying to sneak a peek up our skirts? They tried every trick in the bad boy book to satisfy their inexplicable curiosity about the one thing in life they could never own. I always wondered what the big deal was. If girls are so inferior, why the preoccupation with us?

Those "boys" are now older and have gone on to various venues to continue their irritating habit of obsessing over matters of the skirt set. Some went to work in the name of cause. The more radical went to war in the name of conviction. The really malevolent ones went to Washington where they could do the most damage. But a funny thing happened along the way to legalized misogyny: Hillary Clinton.

Years ago, Sister Mary Ann said it nicely, "Behave yourselves, boys. Don't be mean to the girls." Now Hillary Clinton and a number of other powerful women are sending out the same message. Sister Mary Ann relied on basic goodness to prevail. We are not as blessed. We must rely on the law—fallible as it is—to put teeth in our message.

The Family Leave Act, which provides job security for caregivers (most of whom are women), The Violence Against Women Act, and The Earned Income Tax Credit for the working poor (most of whom are women) are just a few of the accomplishments of a refreshingly pro-woman administration. Enough about reality. Let's talk pulp fiction.

Whitewater. Travelgate. Equality in the workplace. Read: women in the workplace. The current inquisition of Hillary Clinton is not election year entertainment. It's more a Senatorial version of a typically bad episode of *Geraldo*. *Women In Power And The Men Who Hate Them*, hosted by Senator D'Amato.

What is Sister saying now? I'm sure she's quite mortified by this public display of personal pathology, but I bet she's not surprised at the reason for the rage.

Women represent the majority of the workforce, but make no mistake about it, the workplace remains the province of men. For example, nearly two-thirds of all women in the labor force are single, widowed, divorced, or married to men who earn under $15,000 a year. According to the U.S. Department of Labor, the annual median income for women is $16,277 while men earn $26,472. Since the majority of women who work are the sole support of their family, it is no wonder poverty is feminized. Even a woman with a college degree earns less than a man with a high school diploma ($29,609 and $32,137 respectively).

Why? One reason is that women's work is consistently evaluated as inferior. Occupations remain highly segregated with 90% or more of the workers representing one gender. The segregation is almost exclusively economically disadvantageous to women. The low status, pink-collar ghetto of clerical and childcare workers is overpopulated with women. In contrast, over 90% of all airline pilots, dentists, computer scientists, and engineers are men. Even in professions where women have supposedly achieved parity, there is a separate and unequal playing field. Take higher education. Almost 30% of university faculty are female. Encouraging. Until you consider that 62% of those women hold lectureships—the lowest rank in college-level teaching. Translation: little chance of tenure, promotion, or higher salaries. Seventy-five percent of the full professorships are held by white males. The difference in salary is striking. The average annual salary for a male professor is $59,180 while female instructors average $26,390. Aside from the gross waste of talent by underutilizing over half of the human resources we have, there is something inherently wrong with a system that knowingly perpetuates injustice. Is it any surprise that homicide is now the leading cause of death for women in the workplace?

So, what has all of this got to do with Hillary Clinton? Plenty. Even Hillary Clinton, outspoken feminist that she is, knew this country was not ready to accept a woman in the Oval Office. Ultimately, the best she could hope for was the opportunity to exercise her power indirectly through active participation in her husband's work. The glass ceiling remains intact.

Hillary Clinton is a personal reminder to every woman in America of how far we still have to go before we catch even a distant glimpse of true equality. The hostility evoked by one well-educated, highly competent, assertive woman should serve as a wake-up call to all women because it is a microcosm of a larger, more prevalent problem rooted in power and control issues.

Political ideology aside, if Hillary Clinton goes down, we all go down with her. The back of the bus remains in clear view.

—February 26, 1996 *The Tennessee Register*

Author's Note: In 2008, Hillary Rodham Clinton ran for president. Although she did not win, Clinton proved a serious contender, garnering almost eighteen million votes. She was later appointed Secretary of State by President Barack Obama, her one-time rival. As Secretary of State, Clinton served with distinction, traveling to 112 countries during her four-year tenure. She remains a strong advocate for women's rights.

WELFARE REFORM: THE RHETORIC AND THE REALITY

Let me begin by saying I have never received welfare. I have, however, received food stamps, Medicaid (for six months following a leg injury), student loans, federal grants, and Social Security survivor's benefits.

Maybe that's why I do not share the outrage. Been there, done that. And frankly, I don't get it. Why the obsession with welfare reform? Aid To Families With Dependent Children (AFDC), food stamps, and Medicaid combined account for approximately one percent of the federal budget and a little over three percent of our state budget. In terms of dollars and cents, public aid is not a black hole in Uncle Sam's wallet.

So what's the real agenda? The traditional male-dominated family is not coming back. Unless welfare reform mandates Valium in the water supply. The federal deficit is not going to be sharply reduced. Thirty-five year old virgins are not going to represent the majority of women. Minimum wage will not substitute for a minimum standard of living. Removing the marriage penalty, forcing women to take dead-end jobs, and placing a family cap on welfare benefits will not change reality. And the reality is that we live in a two-tier economy that has rendered both the Cleavers and the Calvinistic work ethic obsolete.

Is there a solution, then, to the quagmire of poverty? Amazingly enough, I believe there is. And it has nothing to do with partisan politics. In fact, the first step toward real reform is to stop putting all our problem eggs in a political basket. Policy woven from schemes, self-interest, shifting alliances, and compromise unravels at the first sign of stress. We need something more durable. Less grounded in denial. We need a little compassion. And a commitment to do the right thing. We need a plan based on something other than pain and punishment. We are, contrary to political rhetoric, all in this together. Life remains an eminently non-partisan event.

When I was five-years-old, my parents divorced. My father re-married immediately. It was his third marriage. Two years and one child later, he was divorced again. Eight years later, he died suddenly. He was 51.

Although partially paralyzed from polio, my mother worked part-time as a secretary. She also collected Social Security Disability. And, after he died, I received Dad's Social Security. I also worked six days a week at a bakery to pay for the electric lights and telephone we enjoyed.

After high school, thanks to an assortment of grants, I was able to attend and eventually graduate from college.

Meanwhile, my mother became eligible for energy assistance and food stamps. I often did her grocery shopping. The hostility in the check-out line was almost palpable. Everything I bought was scrutinized. I felt compelled to justify the Pepsi in my cart. The fruit. The soup. It didn't matter. Poverty is so diminishing. It was as if my dignity died with my dad and the paycheck that went with him. I wondered if there would ever be an even playing field. A chance to dream. A way out of the asylum called poverty.

The classroom seemed the only place where things made sense. Hard work and effort led to good grades. Cumulative good grades led to graduation. Graduation led to a better life. So I thought. Instead, graduation led to the Reagan Era. And darkness followed. The age of affluence had arrived.

Today, the distinction between a trauma and no big deal has polarized America. For the record, a trauma is when something bad happens to *us*. No big deal is when something bad happens to *them*. Us vs. them. The haves. The have nots. Trickle down compassion. Priorities, you understand.

We'll bail out the S&L's, but we won't rescue the children. We'll go to war over a cause, but we'll ignore those already here. We'll cut welfare, but we won't aggressively pursue the eight billion owed in back child support. Think how many families would be off welfare if they were given the child support due them. Memo to deadbeat DNA donors: Wake up and smell the latte. Parenting does not end with conception. Kids cost money. Get over yourself and do the right thing. Abandonment is abuse.

There is a Chinese proverb that says to remember is to understand. And I do. I remember the despair and deprivation of poverty. I remember the students who came into my classroom, beneficiaries of the same system that had allowed me to become a professor. I remember the clients I served as a caseworker for the State of Illinois. They—we—all have names. A face. A story. I remember too well. Professionally and personally.

That's why I remain largely unimpressed with social policy shaped by graduates of the *Got Mine, Screw You* School of Economics. I hear the collective groan of an angry public. But then I remember. I remember poverty is more than financial hardship. It is a lifestyle. It's facing real obstacles with limited resources. It's being invisible. Overwhelmed. Powerless. And, now poverty is about partisan redemption.

Poverty is about a lot of things. Reform is not one of them.

—June 3, 1996 *The Tennessee Register*

FAMILIES FIRST, COMPASSION LAST

How did it come to this? When did the poor become the focus of our collective rage? How did welfare reform become synonymous with partisan redemption? When did pain and punishment become the basis of public policy? When did the inmates take over the asylum?

Lots of questions. Serves me right for sleeping through the Eighties. I won't make that mistake again. Okay. I'm awake. I see the handwriting on the wall: America is angry. Make that enraged. Tired of the treadmill. Taxes. Big government. Feminists. The poor. Sex. The usual sundry of evils.

Fortunately, the solution to this cornucopia of angst is coming to Tennessee September 1. That's the day Gov. Don Sunquist's welfare reform package, Families First, will be transformed from Republican rhetoric into Draconian reality.

Families First. Solution in a can. Just add women and children. Stir in minimum "rage" (as my daughter calls it). Garnish with guilt. Serves nothing. Store leftovers in an airtight container of poverty.

This could work. Unless you know better. Then you tend to feel some vague moral obligation to do better. You tend to be bothered by certain discrepancies.

For example, why is the City of New York willing to pay out $22,000 a year to house a mother and her three children in a welfare hotel, but refuses to give her more than $250 a month in rent allowance. City caseworkers know there is no apartment in New York City that rents for $250/month. Unless you consider a roof and walls optional. City administrators know this. Politicians know this. We, the people know this. So what's the *real* agenda? Why are we spending so much money to keep so many people down?

Author and activist Jonathan Kozol offers this explanation: "Two words—'lean' and 'mean' are often used in tandem, and the rhyme appears to resonate with socially attractive implications." Kozol notes a recent trend in applying stringent standards to the poor runs parallel with the cult of fitness that has become an American obsession. Policy, Kozol argues in his book, *Rachel and Her*

Children, has become a metaphor for the solitary runner, turned into a headset that excludes the cries of his less fortunate competitors.

Apparently, our government leaders got a deal on headsets. Bought in bipartisan bulk. Keep out the noise. Maintain the distance between the Beltway and the Safeway. So what if Lamar Alexander didn't know the cost of a gallon of milk or a dozen eggs. If you have to ask how much something costs, you can't afford it. The headset with a mindset. Lean and mean.

How did it come to this? Many of us started out in the same place. Claimed the same zip code. Ate the same generic food. Dreamed the same dreams.

We once sat side by side in crowded classrooms. We listened (even when we pretended to be bored) while teachers preached potential. We believed when they told us we'd one day make a difference. Good thing they didn't mention the role of chance. Or geography. Or that per capita income has a higher correlation with IQ scores than heredity. None of that would have made sense. But that was before the Reagan years. It was before the days of the two-tier economy. Before the Republican Renaissance. Before the days of the rich and the rest of us. Before the great abyss of poverty opened wide enough to swallow whole many of those clinging by a paycheck to the edge.

It was before the "let them eat ketchup" Era. Emphasis on them. And who exactly are them? Twenty-two percent of the poor are children. The ones who eat lead chips while we eat potato chips. Over two-thirds of families headed by women live at or below the poverty line. Minorities are also disproportionately poor. And a small percentage of disabled and elderly receive public aid. All the usual suspects. Low tech nuisances lacking poll power.

Okay. I'm finally getting the drift. Some pigs, as George Orwell noted in *Animal Farm,* are more equal. The family façade first. Children last. Women—don't ask. Just move to the back of the bus. Every window has a view. As Susana Kaysen, author of *Girl, Interrupted* observes, "Every window on Alcatraz has a view of San Francisco." Kaysen was referring to her experience with mental illness. Poverty and mental illness have a lot in common. A sense of helplessness. Hopelessness. Constricted reality. Invisibility. Disdain.

Kaysen says, "People ask, how did you get in there? (referring to her two-year stay in a psychiatric hospital). What they really want to know is if they are likely to end up in there as well. I can't answer the real question. All I can tell them is, it's easy. Reality can be obliterated in the blink of an eye. Or, it can happen in increments." Kaysen describes a series of tiny tears, individually unnoticeable, but taken together create an opening to that place none of us want to visit. And yet, she says, there is a lure to it. Resignation can be very seductive.

A lot like poverty. So swallow down that despair. Smile like a good Stepford wife. And remember, Families First.

—August 11, 1996 *The Tennessean*

ANGER: A NATION AT WAR

Anger. It's been called everything from a powerful tool to right wrongs to the emotional equivalent of an anti-Christ. The fact that psychologists have labeled anger as the most misunderstood emotion is neither coincidence nor understatement.

For better or worse, we are currently a society fueled by high octane anger. Some of it justified, but most of it manufactured as a smoke and mirrors response to a number of dirty little secrets that we collectively work very hard to keep from exposing. In a sense, we are all members of one big dysfunctional family. We have more than the requisite number of symptoms: skyrocketing juvenile crime, a growing underclass, widespread substance abuse, and a prevailing sense of despair about an uncertain future. And, we have Newt Gingrich, the premier symptom of our anger run amok.

Like most dysfunctional families, we also have designated scapegoats: women, children, minorities, and the poor. In short, anyone lacking power, prestige, or purse-strings. The role of blame has been cast, and for the most part is played with Academy Award quality. Some examples: feminists, for their supporting role in the breakdown of the traditional male-dominated family; gangs, for their supporting role in undermining family relationships (granted, it would be a stronger nomination is there were, in fact, relationships to undermine, but we're talking about anger, not accuracy); the media, for their stellar performance in contaminating our otherwise pristine minds with an overdose of sex and violence. God knows we never thought of either until the dawn of television. Last, and certainly least by Republican standards, the poor, for their cameo role of mere existence. "Let them eat cake—as long as it's not part of a free lunch program," defines the Republican platform on social programs for Election Year '96.

Of course, the current menu at the White House Waffle Shop is also growing tedious. Memo to Bill: I know you're trying to hang onto your job (most of us can relate), but this constant pandering to the opposition makes me wonder what kind of syrup is being served with the waffles. Surely that sideshow in San Diego served as a reminder of what happens when you swim with sharks. Even the syrupy-sweet token poster girl skewered you in her keynote speech. Little Suzy bites with the best of them.

P.S. While you're in Chicago, stop by the Henry Horner Housing Project. It's only two blocks from the convention. The other America awaits.

Of course, this epic production in anger would not be possible without the twisted talents of many factors working behind the scenes. Dishonorable mention in this category goes to a truly pathological economic system that simultaneously screams an outdated Calvinistic work ethic while mercilessly beating down those who still affirm the rhetoric.

Hit me, hurt me, but don't leave me—I'm your dwindling dollar. A sick financial relationship is no different from a sick personal relationship. Either way, you're damaged. Casualties are found among divergent family members. For instance, the thirtysomething career woman who chooses to forego motherhood is no different from her fifteen-year-old "sister" who chooses having a child over formal education. Both will bear the anger of society. Neither wins because nobody *can* win in a dysfunctional family. Just ask Susan Smith. Or, if she were still alive, Nicole Brown Simpson.

Finally, no dysfunctional family is complete without its taboos—those "dirty little secrets" I mentioned earlier. What is America's best kept taboo? Simply put, we are a nation at war with itself—this time divided by resources rather than region.

Some battles are fought with words—hate groups espousing ugly rhetoric in the name of the misguided cause of the week; other battles are waged with punitive social policies designed to further disenfranchise the weakest links of the human chain. Skirmishes are fought passively with mind-numbing drugs, an increase in suicide, and this sense of collective anger that is quickly building to a blind rage directed at virtually anybody who crosses our path.

Women feel resentful and exploited. Men feel confused and unappreciated. Teens feel pessimistic and overwhelmed. Minorities feel oppressed. Whites feel guilty (at least those of us with a conscience do) and scared. Conservatives feel cheated. Liberals feel threatened. Gays feel defensive. Heterosexuals feel numb. Teachers feel powerless. Parents feel helpless. Anger appears to be the only tie binding our collective family.

Worse than a dysfunctional family, we are a disconnected family. For example, a recent study by psychologist Gary Melton revealed disturbing images of American life: 40 percent of Melton's almost 2,000 subjects answered "nothing," when asked what, if anything, they had done during the past one year for a child other than their own. The majority of these same subjects identified violent crime as the number one problem facing America today. Self-absorption rears its ugly head.

Subjects were also asked who they would turn to in a crisis. Respondents from large urban areas said they would hire a professional listener (e.g., a psychiatrist), or if unable to rent-a-friend, would go to a hospital emergency room. The majority of subjects from rural communities said, "no one." None of the subjects, rich or poor, listed family, neighbors, or clergy.

Sounds like it's time to transcend our collective anger and figure out a way to call off this uncivil war.

—August 26, 1996 *The Tennessee Register*

BLESSED ARE THE INSURED, FOR THEY SHALL BE HEALED

As I write this, rows of cardboard boxes surround me. I have packed the contents of all 119 boxes personally. The past and present, stacked and packed. Never has my chaotic life looked so organized. And finalized. All in less than thirty days. All because a routine trip to Target and an unexpected phone call colluded to change the course of my life.

It began in the parking lot, actually. I had glanced across the access road to check for oncoming traffic. That's when the bright streams of color in the adjacent woods caught my eye. I slowed down to take a closer look. And then, from the safety of my sedan, I got a glimpse of a parallel universe. Faces of the other America.

A makeshift shelter. A frayed clothesline strung across two barrels. Clothes blowing in the mild winter wind. A filthy mattress. Litter strewn about. And, at the nearby exit ramp, other residents of the cardboard community stood. Soliciting money from passing motorists. How did it come to this, I wonder.

I pry my upwardly mobile offspring from her *Goosebumps* book and force her to look into the eye of the tiger. I want her to see reality. I want her to develop a social conscience about the human condition. And, I want her to do what my generation could or would not do—fix it.

She closes her book. Perennial life lessons. An occupational hazard for children of former professors.

Does she realize that between 2-3 million people are currently homeless in America? That the face of homelessness circa 1997 is a white, thirtysomething, single mother with two children under the age of five? No child support. No social network. No government safety net. No home. But for the grace of God, she is me.

It reminds me of the water exhibit we saw recently at the museum. Tanks of good, fair, and contaminated water containing fish and other indigenous marine life were on display. The fish in the contaminated water were drab and sluggish. Lethargic. Hopeless.

Conversely, the fish in the good water appeared vibrant and energetic. The fish in the fair water coped.

The three tanks were positioned so the unlucky occupants of the contaminated water had a clear view of their counterparts thriving in the nearby, but totally segregated good water. Just like poverty. Every window has a view. Especially when you're on the outside looking in.

Hours later, Nova races into my office announcing, "Daddy's on the phone" and "he needs to talk to you immediately." As if the sky is falling. Six-year-olds. So histrionic.

The conversation is terse. The firm has folded. Permanent layoffs. Effective immediately. One month's severance pay. And then the really bad news: all benefits, including health and dental insurance, pension, and profit-sharing are also terminated. Effective immediately. The unsinkable company has sunk. Quicker than you can say *Dilbert*.

Suddenly, I am one of them again. The uninsured. Unprotected. And unfunded.

The next two weeks pass in a flurry of updating resumes, cold calls, and interviews. For him. A cautionary note: motherhood is not a marketable skill. Unless you wear a crown.

Meanwhile, Nova develops a cough that sounds worse with each passing day. I pray it will go away. And that we'll have insurance again. Me and 37 million other Americans (including 10 million kids like my daughter).

Another week passes. Notices to disconnect the phone and utilities arrive. The car payment is way overdue. And a notice to vacate (read: eviction) is taped on the front door. Another day in poverty paradise.

Nova is now coughing late into the night. It sounds more biting, harsher. And persistent. Late one night, she appears in my bedroom. "Mommy, I'm really sick. I think it's time we take me to the doctor."

Earth to Beltway: Exactly who is running the asylum? When did the wealth maintenance organization take over? When did pain and profit become inextricably bound? Blessed are the insured, for they shall be healed. All others pay cash. Or die. The American way.

How many times must the parents of 10 million children listen helplessly to the cries of their sick offspring before you finally take a stand and say with campaign-quality certitude, "enough"?

Time to mandate universal health care coverage. Time to make the finest medical care in the world both available and accessible to everyone, regardless of 1040 status. Time at last, to do the right thing.

Finally, a job offer. Even an increase in salary. A window with a better view. And a new life down the road. Literally.

Nova's cough (which eventually became my cough) finally went away after spending over $200 on doctor's visits and prescriptions. Thanks to the new job, I had the money.

Still, thirty days of life in the other America is a sobering reminder that poverty and peace of mind do not mix. Nobody should ever have to ask, "At what price, my life." As a nation, we know better. Now we need to do better. Anything less is a sin against humanity. And eminently tragic.

—May 5, 1997 *The Tennessee Register*

BELTWAY BARBIE MEETS KEN (STARR)

"Mom, what's going on with my Barbie dolls?" asked my 7-year-old daughter. Handing me a recent copy of *Newsweek*, Nova pointed to the article containing the disturbing news.

"The article says they're going to change Barbie and make her look more real. Why do they want to make her real? Now Ken won't want to date her anymore. She'll just be ordinary—*yuk*."

Hello Mattel? Political correctness is a nice idea, but seven-year-olds aren't exactly impressed with reality. Children, including the majority of males under 85, like fantasy. An inverse relationship between brain and bra size. A thick mane of honey blonde, perfectly coiffed hair. And a way cool, color-coordinated wardrobe that screams, "take me, I'm easy." Personality optional.

Take the latest scandal at 1600. When the story first broke, Nova and I were watching our favorite afternoon soap, which was admittedly becoming very predictable. The reason? Reality had reared its ugly head in almost all the intertwined plots. Having Peter Jennings break the monotony with a 'true' melodrama was actually a welcome respite from contrived reality.

And not just because of the lurid content (although if this and previous allegations are true, one guy is really upsetting the law of supply and demand for everyone else). Like most of America, I've become so desensitized to scandal, it would take a moral outrage of the first magnitude to rattle me—say my daughter suddenly announcing that she's a Republican.

No, the real shock was my daughter's disturbing reaction to the breaking news of power and passion gone awry at the White House.

"Wow," said Nova, her eyes wide with astonishment, "Monica's parents must be so proud of her—having sex with the President is a *big* accomplishment. I mean, he's the smartest most powerful man in the whole world."

Once the blood resumed flowing in my brain, I made a feeble attempt to explain the meaning of "alleged." As if it mattered. My pint-sized pundit had innocently, yet succinctly spoken for most of adult America that day.

Wink, wink. Let's get on with our lives. And prosperity. What's reality got to do with the price of cappuccino? Or a good fantasy?

Frankly, I agree with the id gang. Why fix the guys and dolls if they're not broken? Which brings me back to Barbie. If making Barbie appear more realistic is the true goal, a change of persona, not proportion is called for.

For example, instead of those annoyingly cheerful utterances ("let's go shopping" and "math is hard") every Brain Dead Barbie is programmed to recite, the new, realistic version—we'll call her Beltway Barbie—would state forcefully (but with a hint of coyness), "sexual harassment is wrong" or (smugly) "I'm invoking the Fifth Amendment in this matter."

Beltway Barbie's updated wardrobe would still include the traditional line of Victoria's Secret career apparel, a power suit and flats for those rare moments spent on her feet, and a roll of easy-to-remove adhesive tape (securely holds wire in place with minimal chaffing).

But instead of the usual sundry accessories, Beltway Barbie would feature far more realistic accouterments: inflatable resume, miniature wire and blank audiotapes. Refillable subpoena pads and literary agent also available. Ken (Starr) sold separately.

Let's face it. Reality is overrated. Pedestrian. And not very marketable. No one would buy Beltway Barbie. Would they? Surely savvy consumers know a dud when they see one. Just another sales pitch. So ordinary. Mundane. And eminently boring. Obviously a right-wing conspiracy.

However, other equally realistic (but more entertaining) versions of Barbie might prove marketable. Included would be such perennial favorites as:

1) PMS Barbie, a salt and sugar craving babe with an attitude. PMS Barbie would feature an expandable wardrobe, water retention, and a bag of Hershey miniatures. Gun sold separately.

2) Chemically Content Barbie, a Prozac-wielding good-time girl who comes with a couch and a past. Insight sold separately.

3) A special-edition Binge and Purge Barbie available in three sizes: before, during, and after dinner. Comes with a calorie counter and includes

instructions on proper purging etiquette. Laxatives sold separately.

4) Twelve-step Barbie praying the serenity prayer and poised for the secret handshake. Co-dependent Skipper not sold separately.

The possibilities are endless (Psychotic Barbie, Dysfunctional Family Barbie, Work-Release Barbie, etc.) and infinitely more appealing than "physically proportionate" Barbie. Or Beltway Barbie. Just ask Ken. Or Bill.

—February 28, 1998 *The Dispatch*

THE RAGE AND ROUTINE OF AMERICA—ONE YEAR LATER

Another sleepless night. Followed by the promise of another dreary day. It is a routine I am all too familiar with as I struggle out of bed early on the morning of September 11, 2001. A messy divorce, health problems, financial struggles—all the usual suspects of a midlife gone awry left me mired in self-pity most days. And feeling incredibly alone.

Little do I know that four jets and thousands of innocent victims are about to glue a nation of incredibly alone and angst-driven people together in such a profound way that every problem, whether petty or insurmountable, will suddenly be redefined. Every priority and routine re-evaluated. Every belief and bias questioned.

My then ten-year-old daughter, Nova, and I arrive at MTSU late that morning. After seeing the televised horror, she had asked if we could stop at McDonald's for hot cakes and orange juice. Advantage childhood. Food first. Fear later.

In class, I tell my unusually somber students that America has been brutally assaulted by a band of faceless thugs. And the trauma of that violent act will live with us forever. We have lost our innocence. Now we must find our forgiveness.

We discuss the reasons for this vile act. The struggle for power and dominance. The voracious hatred and rage that led to this crime of grand proportion. And, unfortunately, the role we Americans unwittingly play in this epic jihad.

My students are so young. So idealistic. So uncomfortable with the notion that we are the focal point of unbelievable rage around the globe. The 'Ugly American' is not a familiar concept to this generation.

When one of my students who lived in Saudi Arabia for five years recounts stories of public beheadings, decapitation, zealotry, and horrible retribution for "crimes" such as adultery (alleged or real), my students are stunned speechless. They, like most of America, can't begin to grasp the magnitude of difference that separates the Christian and Islamic world. But on this day, they have watched those two worlds collide in a way that will forever change the face and future of America.

One month after 9-11, I invite a guest speaker from Syria to visit my classes. My students are initially wary of the veiled woman who speaks with great conviction about her life as a Muslim. And her view of Christ (he's just the second of three great prophets, according to the Koran) does not set well with my conservative Southern Baptist students. But as the hour passes, our speaker also speaks graciously of commonalities with Christians (e.g., the desire for peace and justice), other women (wanting a good education for all our children) and Westerners, in general (shopping for sales at the mall). One small step.

A few weeks later, Nova and I take a "field trip" to an Islamic marketplace in Nashville. We want—need to learn. It is not a comfortable venue for two scantily dressed (by Arab standards) American females to be in the aftermath of 9-11. But it is a necessary place to be. How else can we learn? And sometimes, hearts in the right place do prevail.

A colorful chunk of Moroccan candy that catches Nova's eye and a mom that's always asking questions leads to meeting the owner of the market. I tell him that we've come to learn about the Islamic way of life. And I apologize for not having my head covered. It is my choice, he tells me politely. His tone suggests my choice is not the right one. Still, he seems pleased that we'd made the effort and tells Nova to take the candy as his gift to her. Another small step.

That afternoon, Nova emerges from her room with a shoebox transformed into a Red Cross donation box and proceeds to solicit money from neighbors, her Girl Scout troop, and everyone else who crosses her path in the next week. She just wants to help, she says. Spontaneous altruism. Another step in the right direction.

In the months that follow 9-11, I watch with sadness as my once carefree students evolve into grim young adults worrying about anthrax, the possibility of a reinstated draft, dying in a country many can't locate on a map for a cause they barely understand. And then it's time for finals and flights home. Sixteen weeks and one lifetime have passed since we first met at the beginning of the semester.

And now, here we are one year later. The journey that we as a classroom and nation were collectively forced to take when fate and hate collided one unforgettable Tuesday morning has revealed more than a path of pain. It has also been a journey of small steps toward enlightenment and empathy. Love and letting go. Lost innocence and forgiveness. Hope and healing. And the journey continues…

—September 11, 2002 *The Daily News Journal*

THE RED ZONE: FOREIGN CORRESPONDENT ANNE GARRELS REFLECTS ON LIFE IN POST-WAR IRAQ

The Green Zone—four square miles of heavily fortified 'safe' ground in Baghdad. The Red Zone—everything else. A friendly Iraqi translator named Amer. The infamous Palestine Hotel. Watching Marines receive intravenous injections of saline to avoid dehydration before fighting insurgents in the 130-degree desert heat. A gorgeous journalist named Ivan who must dye his blond hair 'Baghdad brown' to fit in with the populace. A young American soldier who has retrofitted the plastic doors of his jeep with pieces of his own flak jacket. Ukrainian soldiers reporting for duty in tennis shoes, dragging ancient vehicles that won't run. The 'Coalition of the Willing.'

Two hours of electricity followed by six hours without power. Repeat cycle. Water best described as 'discolored.' Keeping a very low profile. Always riding in the back seat of a battered Toyota, not a Black SUV that screams, "shoot me" (which they do). Always hiding behind a burqa and chador that renders women invisible both in fact and symbol. Understanding the depth of tradition and tribalism that defines daily life in Iraq.

Avoiding convoys, Fallujah, and bad timing.

These are the sights and sounds that define the difficult days and treacherous nights of Anne Garrels, National Public Radio's senior foreign correspondent stationed in Baghdad, Iraq.

Garrels, one of sixteen American non-embedded journalists who remained in Baghdad during the American invasion of Iraq, has written a powerful narrative, *Naked In Baghdad*, which chronicles the dreary days leading up to the war, the actual invasion, and immediate aftermath. *Naked In Baghdad* is a must read for anyone who takes a ballot seriously, knows a soldier, or even remotely cares about the quagmire that we currently find ourselves in halfway across the globe.

Selected by Middle Tennessee State University as its Summer Reading pick (for the past three years, incoming freshman are assigned a book to read that has broad appeal across disciplines), *Naked In Baghdad* provides readers a series of vivid and disturbing snapshots of war and its ugly aftermath. Stripping away the layers of political posturing/propaganda/philosophizing that characterize most discussions about Iraq these days, Garrels also manages to present an intelligent and informed view of the Iraq invasion and occupation.

On Sunday, Garrels, back in the U.S. briefly (she returns to Iraq in October), was the keynote speaker at Middle Tennessee State University's Convocation (the official kickoff event for the academic year). The night before, Garrels spoke at the Linebaugh Library, providing an updated look at life in post-war Iraq (*Naked In Baghdad* concludes in May, 2003) along with an incisive commentary about the "mistakes" made by our current administration regarding the war.

"Dumb mistakes," Garrels emphasizes. Mistakes such as "ostracizing the Baathists, underestimating how much Iraqis would resent foreign occupation, ignoring the deeply embedded traditions and tribalism among Iraqis, neutralizing the Iraqi military and police, killing huge numbers of Iraqi civilians, and denying persistent rumors about widespread prisoner abuse at Abu Ghraib until the situation was way out of hand have brought Iraq to the threshold of a full-blown civil war" that, according to Garrels, is now all but unavoidable.

Garrels recalls her translator, Amer, telling her with great sadness that his life, although difficult under Saddam, now resembles a mirror that has been shattered and can't be put back together.

Every day, thousands of shattered lives like Amer's intersect with fanaticism and a foreign flag. The result is deadly. The solutions elusive. And the hope all but gone.

Although her insights and vivid impressions from ground zero of a war torn country cast a harsh light on this chapter of American history, Garrels underscores that she is proud to be an American and believes we can do better. The question is whether we will.

In the meantime, Garrels frenetic lifestyle—schlepping back and forth from her home in suburban Connecticut to her tiny house in

Baghdad's Red Zone—promises more stories. And a glimpse into a larger truth than politics can handle.

BACK TO SCHOOL
WITHOUT PETER JENNINGS

I am not a good Catholic. I've known this for a long time, mainly because devout Catholic readers tell me so every time I write a column about anything remotely religious.

So, over the years, I've learned to dial it down a notch, unless it really, really matters. And as I get older, less matters. The Catholic Church and their 'rules' predate me by two millennia and will still be around long after I'm just a memory to my offspring.

That's why last April, when all hope of reform went up in white smoke, philosophical disappointment was quickly overshadowed by a practical relief—black smoke might have delayed my daughter's upcoming Confirmation (these things matter when you're a parent).

Now we've met the new boss, same as the old boss, as the song goes. Perhaps a little more detached. Less diplomatic. And not quite the showstopper his predecessor was. But, essentially cut from the same clerical cloth—all dogma, no debate. Which means even more divisiveness. More strident views. More institutional insufferableness. More dilution of the faith. And more attrition from the pew and polls. Somewhat like the results of the last presidential election.

Which sadly brings me to the recent death of ABC News anchor Peter Jennings, the premier calming voice of our turbulent times.

Every night at exactly 5:30 P.M., Peter Jennings dispassionately delivered what no pope or president appears capable of—a balanced picture of the world and the major events shaping our lives.

With an impressive blend of reason and rhetoric, Peter Jennings both informed and inspired his audience about the larger world—no easy feat in this day of express lane views and values. And it's the main reason this Hollywood-handsome, Canadian-born anchorman's legacy of integrity will remain relevant long after popes and presidents fade into history.

So another school year begins, sans an unmet, but beloved colleague. Back to school without Peter Jennings (we concluded every day of homeschool for the last ten years by listening to and then discussing *World News Tonight*) is a dreary prospect.

But then it's been a dreary decade—perfectly illustrated late on Election Night 2004 with Peter Jennings seated at his newsdesk in front of a map of the United States hemorrhaging red. Just behind him, a lone blue holdout—Illinois—stood out like a beacon of hope against a foregone conclusion. An unexpected pang of homesickness for my Yankee (read: Democrat) roots hit at that moment—the first I've experienced in two decades of living in Dixie. Then Peter Jennings must have said something brilliant because the moment passed.

But not the memory—that night was a turning point in every way that matters. Politically, historically, socially—the jagged landscape of life has changed dramatically in recent months. And now there is no steady voice to put it all in perspective. Both Peter Jennings and the fleeting hope for a change in regime that defined that night are now a part of history.

While searching various websites for a photo of my favorite news anchor (good Catholics, unlike me, have pictures of the Pope, not Peter Jennings on their wall), I was further saddened to read how not having graduated high school haunted Peter Jennings all his life. How ironic—this sophisticated, urbane man of the world who brought so much information into our lives felt bad about not having a piece of paper. Add humility to the list of characteristics that further distinguished Peter Jennings from the rest of the pack.

And so the dashing foreign correspondent turned news anchor who put some much needed global sparkle into the lives of millions of viewers will be sorely missed.

Our homeschool social studies class—my daughter grew up watching major news events unfold on *World News Tonight* —and the larger world is less informed tonight, and without Peter Jennings in it, maybe even a little less interesting.

As I said, I am not a good Catholic. But I'm still saying a rosary for Peter Jennings.

—August 21, 2005 *The Huntsville Times*

THE SEASON OF HATE

Not long ago, a small group of protesters touting snippets of Scripture and wielding signs that read "God Hates America" and "Thank God For Dead Soldiers" arrived in Smyrna, Tennessee, to disrupt the funeral of Staff Sergeant Asbury F. Hawn II, the town's most recent casualty of war in Iraq.

After unleashing months of intense heat and humidity throughout the South, it seems summer has finally surrendered to an even more oppressive opponent—the season of hate that follows members of the controversial Westboro Baptist Church, based in Topeka, Kansas, across America.

They come to grief-stricken towns burying fallen soldiers to spread their doomsday message that America is "irreversibly and eternally damned." They come especially to small towns, where they will get the most notice.

Everywhere from Peoria, Illinois to Opelika, Alabama to Duluth, Minnesota, to Smyrna, Tennessee. And, on Labor Day weekend, even Sweden (King Gustav and his subjects are doomed to a particularly vile ending, according to the church's website) was the recipient of this group's vitriolic vision and mission.

They get around (deep pockets underwriting the extensive travel?). And, predictably, enrage large numbers of otherwise peaceful people.

"Hope your plane crashes" and "Burn in hell" are the only printable epitaphs shouted by the large crowd of locals that formed in a parking lot across the street from the Smyrna lot occupied by Saturday's picketers, who themselves totaled less than a dozen.

Unfazed and completely outnumbered by the local residents heckling them, the picketers continued their antics for one very long hour, including kicking a large American flag back and forth, and then stomping on it.

"You're going to just let her kick the flag around like that," a middle-aged man angrily demanded as he made his way across the street and stood within a few feet of the protestors, cordoned off from the crowd in a separate parking lot.

One of the four police officers stationed in front of the lot shook his head, "It's their constitutional right to do so, sir." Growing more agitated, the man again implored the officer to make her stop. The officer patiently repeated that it was their right, "just like it's your group's right to protest over there."

The flag was gleefully kicked about several more times, and with increasing enthusiasm. It was, admittedly, disturbing to watch.

Then, suddenly, the picketers were hustled into two waiting cars and given a police escort out of town. Their one-hour permit to protest had expired, just minutes before the funeral procession for Staff Sergeant Hawn would pass by.

Undaunted by the growing rage and heckling of townspeople, the picketers continued to smile and wave from the safety of their cars.

As the caravan passed within a few feet of where I stood, it was obvious the car's occupants were high on hate—giddy from the misery they'd inflicted on a small town in mourning. Even more disturbing was the look of complete certitude on their faces. They are 100 percent certain they're right, I realized. And there's no arguing with righteousness. End of story.

Well, not quite. To fully appreciate the magnitude of this group's caustic message, you need to visit their website. But be forewarned—these people hate you and you *will* feel it.

For example, I decided to listen to one of Pastor Fred Phelps' recent online sermons, which ironically was on the subject of the "creative class." According to Pastor Phelps, as a member of the media, "the perverted press," I am damned to hell (sorry, sir, I'm already there—ever tried to make a living as a writer?) and that because "every editorial decision promotes Satan's Big Lie," God hates me. So have a nice day.

At least they are equal opportunity haters—gays (public enemy number one, according to their website), 'adulterers', mainstream ministers ("no better than modern day Pharisees"), the press, the military, "Pervert Bush and Pervert Clinton" (no red and blue division with this group) are all loathed by them. They do not, however, hate African-Americans and want to make it clear that they are not racist. Good to know.

Space and sensibility prevent me from elaborating more about this little group of hate mongers who, in addition to picketing the funerals of dead soldiers, proudly announce "Thank God For Katrina" (you can imagine why they're glad to see the Big Easy slide into the Gulf of Mexico) as well as other natural and manmade disasters on their website.

Their website, www.godhatesfags.com says it all. And unfortunately, more. May the season of hate pass quickly.

—September 11, 2005 *The Huntsville Times*

Part Four
Notes From A Restless Heart
In Perpetual Motion

TO LIVE AND DIE IN PARADISE

It was the stuff of miracles: last minute, spontaneous, and against all odds. Vintage Shalynn.

My one-size-fits-all dreams hero once again pulling off an incredible feat. Suddenly, a tragic mistake was transformed into a magical memory. Quicker than you can say Aloha.

The 'mistake' began months ago when my long distance sweetie first told me he'd been invited to speak about his book in Hawaii. I had enthusiastically (so I thought) indicated that I'd like to go along.

It would be an expensive trip, he said. So, I didn't press. I didn't want to be a burden. He thought my enthusiasm had waned. I thought I was being polite. He said. She said. A few more fights. More time passed. Then the shocking news: he was going to Hawaii. Alone. For a month. Without me. How did we get to this place?

Ever since I was ten-years-old and fell head over heels in love with the handsome, suave and ever stylishly dressed Steve McGarrett ("book 'em, Dan-o") of *Hawaii Five-O* fame, I have dreamed of seeing the sandy beaches and swaying palms of Oahu. It was my fondest dream. And now, *he* was going to live *my* dream. It was a tragic mistake of cosmic proportion. But, hey, it's reality. So I told myself.

He called frequently. Hawaii was lackluster, he reported dejectedly. "What do you expect?" I shot back. "You're on your honeymoon without your wife. You're alone in the most romantic place on Earth—with only the memory of a 'dead' wife for company. Of course, it's 'lackluster.'" Dramatic statements. A writer's forte.

The second week brought no relief. For either of us. Lackluster became dreary. Dismal. And finally dreadful. For both of us.

"Is there any way—any way at all—that I can come over there?" I pleaded one Sunday afternoon. The high water mark of misery had come earlier that day while sitting in Mass contemplating the meaning of my self-imposed hell. Pride goeth before the fall. And I was falling. Fast.

We had made a mistake. Many in recent months. But this was one mistake we could still fix. How often does that happen? Besides, if we knew we would be dead one year from today, would we let anything keep us from being together today? More dramatic statements. Straight from a desperate heart.

He said he'd think about it. No guarantees. Still, I was confident. A door had just opened. And my foot was firmly in it.

Less than an hour later, the phone rang. Could I leave on Thursday morning for Honolulu?

He met me at the airport in Hilo, on the 'big island' of Hawaii. The magic man that made a ten-year-old girl's lifelong dream come true. And gave a grown-up girl paradise on a plate. All expenses paid.

Volcanoes. Mountains. Deserts. Exotic jungles with lush vegetation. Tropical fruit trees. Romantic white sand beaches that serve as backdrops for movies like *South Pacific*, where Mitzi Gaynor vowed to "wash that man right out of my hair."

Hawaiian and Polynesian food (cheap and incredibly tasty). Lodging at a banyan tree-lined resort overlooking the Pacific Ocean. Learning about tsunamis (tidal waves). Strolling through quaint villages. Mass at a beautiful church rebuilt after Hurricane Iniki unleashed her fury in 1991.

Lighthouses. Ocean liners floating along the pink horizon at Waikiki beach. Soothing rains (no thunder or lightning). Exotic island beauties dressed in tropical print sarong dresses. Kauai Pie Ice Cream. And did I mention the romance? Paradise perfect.

Our last day in Hawaii found us at Pearl Harbor. It was a sobering contrast with the frivolity of our past week.

Staring across the peaceful ocean toward the palm tree-lined shore, listening to the sounds of exotic birds calling to one another, watching the sun serenely reflect off the turquoise water, I imagine that fateful Sunday morning in 1941. Just another day in paradise, the doomed sailors of the Arizona must have thought. Until death filled the sky. And a naïve nation learned that even paradise isn't exempt from profound pain.

That's the eerie, paradoxical quality about Pearl Harbor. It is a place of war. And peace. A place of death and despair. And hope. Eternal rest. And eternal turmoil. A place not easily forgotten.

We left Hawaii in a somber mood. Pearl Harbor—and the miracle that brought us there together—were dramatic reminders of the fragility of life. Love. And even paradise.

—March 30, 1999 The Dispatch

BAHAMAS ON A BUDGET: NOT IF YOU PLAN TO EAT

So there's a tax refund check burning a hole in your pocket. What to do? Pay off some medical bills? Pay down a credit card? Put a down payment on a better car?

Of course we did the responsible thing: planned a new, tighter budget while on a flight to the Bahamas.

Blame it on my eleven-year-old daughter, Nova, a seasoned traveler who originally spotted the dirt-cheap fares advertised at a local travel agency.

It seemed like an incredible deal—$279 for four nights in the Bahamas (airfare, hotel room, airport transfers, tax, and gratuities incl.). Kids under 12 Free, if traveling before August 27th. Everything except food. *Caveat emptor.*

So, like lambs led to slaughter, we found ourselves on a flight to Freeport, the capital of Grand Bahama Island, and home to more hustlers per square mile than Vegas. Ironically, a drunken tourist from Idaho would sum it up best when he slurred a sobering truth on our shuttle bus, "Just remember folks, there ain't nothin' 'free' about Freeport."

Our flight and hotel check-in (a recently renovated Holiday Inn SunSpree) were remarkably uneventful. Perfect weather (it was peak hurricane season) also graced our path.

But then it was time to eat. A light supper (two hamburgers, a small conch salad and an iced-tea shared by all three of us) at the Bavarian Beer Gardens set us back $28.00. At $3.00, the fresh conch (pronounced "conk") salad, a tasty concoction of conch meat, lime juice, diced onions, tomatoes, and sweet peppers, was the best value on the menu.

Still, gluttonous Americans accustomed to super-size everything and unlimited free drink refills may find small portions (a 12-ounce drink is considered standard. The Big Gulp doesn't exist in the Bahamas. Except when the bill arrives.) combined with high prices difficult to swallow. Plus, a 15% gratuity is always added into restaurant tabs at the front end. That way, waiters aren't stiffed by light-weights who can't handle their 150-proof Jamaican rum. Unsus-pecting tourists like us who leave a tip on the table pay twice.

Since we don't consume alcohol, and the water was tolerable, sodas—at $2.00-3.00 each, were quickly dismissed as unnecessary luxuries. Until we found a Subway across town where we could sneak back to the soda machine and refill our shared drink cup. Of course, we paid dearly for the privilege of brackish-tasting soda (manufactured in Nassau, it has a very different taste than Ameri-cans are used to).

So we became Junkanoo junkies. Junkanoo Punch tastes like pineapple juice with a twist of 7-Up and something else we couldn't identify (probably heroin) that made the non-alcoholic concoction positively addictive.

To save money, we rode the bus everywhere, including down-town to the Winn Dixie grocery store to stock up on food at local prices (we were, after all, experienced travelers).

Turns out grocery shopping was a wasted effort. Virtually no food is grown in the Bahamas. Hence, nearly everything edible must be imported from big brother to the north. And there is a huge duty added to imports. Which is then passed on to both impoverished locals (everybody I interviewed said they had to work at least two—if not three—jobs to survive) and their American counterparts.

And then there's the matter of credit cards. Most moderately priced (a relative term, to be sure) eating establishments do not ac-cept credit cards. The more pricey venues were out of our budget. For example, we could have dined at our hotel and charged it, but our meals would soon exceed the cost of our airfare. Another hotel restaurant offered ala carte options, but appetizers started at twenty dollars. The idea was to have a relaxing vacation on a budget, not max out another credit card.

A Pizza Hut (credit cards welcome) four blocks from our hotel offered renewed hope that we might yet again eat more than a snack. But hope was short-lived. To get to Pizza Hut, we had to walk a gauntlet of aggressive street vendors and hustlers that cruise the boulevards and parking lots. Sidewalk scams included offers of drugs, "partying," hair braiding, spiritual guidance, and other, less printable services.

After trudging three blocks, we grew weary of dodging both relentless hustlers and motorists driving on the left side of the road (throwback to the days of British occupation) at speeds that would rattle even the most adventurous American. It's no surprise that traffic fatalities are the second leading cause of death among tourists (starvation is number one—okay, it's really drowning, but starvation has to be in the top five).

On Sunday morning, we walked to Mary, Star of the Sea Catholic Church and attended Mass. The lengthy (two hours), but inspiring service featured Calypso music and more congregation enthusiasm than I've ever witnessed at home. The fellowship and friendliness of the congregation, freely given (unlike the food we were always searching for), left us feeling spiritually nourished. It was the highpoint of our trip.

The next day, as we were leaving Subway (where else?), a street vendor offered to braid Nova's hair. She looked at us expectantly— a colorful hair wrap was within reach. If all her spending money hadn't been used for something as mundane as food.

But we'd learned to haggle. Relentlessly. Until the unbelievable bargain price of $5.00 was reached and a softhearted stepdad reached into his pocket and produced his absolute last five-dollar bill (saved back for an emergency—like this).

The next morning, we packed and headed to the airport with our scant souvenirs and stash of Junkanoo Punch. A few pounds lighter for the return flight. And a few miles wiser about bargains that don't include incidentals like food.

—October 13, 2002 *The Tullahoma News*
—October 21, 2002 *The Daily News Journal*

THE BIG EASY YOU DON'T KNOW:
LAISSEZ LES BON TEMPS ROULER

In 1803, Thomas Jefferson bought 800,000 square miles of land from the French government for the unbelievably low price of $15 million (about four cents an acre). The Louisiana Purchase, *aka* the best red, er, blue light real estate special ever, will be hosting a variety of activities and events during the coming year to celebrate its bicentennial milestone.

Best of all, the bargain basement deals that began with Jefferson and Napoleon negotiating the Louisiana Purchase continues to this day. Especially if you're lucky enough to live anywhere near a city served by Southwest Airlines. Recent airfares from either Birmingham or Nashville to New Orleans have hit rock bottom—under fifty bucks each way. So there's no excuse not to head to the French Quarter.

A word to the wise: New Orleans never sleeps, but if you want to, you'll need accommodations. And since the cost of a hotel room in the French Quarter or any other tony address can easily exceed airfare, it's best to negotiate your hotel room price before booking a flight. Research "Daylight Savings" promos, off-peak rates, and inquire about the coupons offered by major credit card companies (we used a combination of all three to get our final deal). That way, you can sleep cheap in the Big Easy and save your money for what really matters: food, fun, and schlock.

A good pair of walking shoes and the ability to hop a streetcar to faraway places such as the Garden District (chic antique stores, stunning antebellum homes, and trendy restaurants) and Riverfront/Zoo/Aquarium area eliminate the need for a car in New Orleans. Another expense averted.

There is much more to do in New Orleans than any three-day, belated honeymoon trip could ever encompass, but we did manage to sample a few local dishes (the seafood gumbo and Creole sausage pizza at Arnaud's Remoulade on Bourbon Street were perfect inaugural snacks for the uninitiated—spiced to maim, not kill your taste buds), visit the Audubon Aquarium of the Americas (discount coupons found in the New Orleans Visitor's Guide—available at hotel desk), scour various shops in the French Quarter to negotiate our own version of the Louisiana Purchase (hands down, the best deals on t-shirts, voodoo dolls, and general New Orleans memorabilia were found at the C-N Gift Center on Decatur Street), and even pass within a few feet of actor Gene Hackman filming a street scene for the upcoming movie, *Runaway Jury*.

And then we came upon Bourbon Street, where the motto is, "Laissez les bon temps rouler." Translation: let the good times roll. And it does. Around the clock. Year around.

Although impossible not to gawk at the sheer bawdiness of endless noisy bars featuring gargantuan-sized drinks like the Hurricane and Hand Grenade, strip clubs, sex toy outlets, and schlock shops, Bourbon Street is definitely not suitable for audiences under 18—or those of any age with either a sense of modesty or preference for a non-smoking section (pungent cigar smoke, as well as other, more obnoxious odors hang heavy in the night air). Still, there is a perverted charm about such open decadence. Three extra Hail Mary's at the nearby St. Louis Cathedral (the oldest in the nation) for those of us who don't have the willpower to skip the Big Sleazy side of New Orleans.

Although Mardi Gras (Latin for Fat Tuesday) and Bourbon Street often eclipse the kinder, gentler side of New Orleans, our late autumn experience of the Crescent City (so named for its location on the bend of the Mississippi River) was mellow and mild. A long way from the noise and naughtiness that will resume in the spring. And a much less humid version (average daily temperature in November is 70 degrees).

The soothing sounds of zydeco, jazz, and soulful blues music playing on every street corner. World-class cuisine served with a seductive Southern charm that would make Blanche DuBois blush. A place of mystery (the famous above-ground cemeteries—"Cities of the Dead", voodoo dolls, and tales of ghosts and goblins) that haunts the imagination. The sinful sugariness of the famous beignet (French doughnuts served hot and sweet at the Café Du Monde). The eccentric street artisans that entertain for donations and distinction—it does, after all, take a certain amount of moxie to perform one's craft in the shadow of legends. All of these are part of the allure of New Orleans. And the reason I'm going back. Soon.

—December 15, 2002 *The Tullahoma News*

—December 15, 2002 *The Dispatch*

NASHVILLE ON THE CHEAP: AN INSIDER'S PERSPECTIVE

Relocating to Tennessee from Illinois nearly sixteen years ago was an easy transition for me. Between visiting Nashville regularly since childhood and a ton of kin already living here, I understood the five basic rules of Yankee survival in the South:

1. Always serve the best meal you can for Sunday supper. It's a matter of personal honor. And the reason non-believing spouses are willing to endure two-hour church services.

2. A can of good hair spray (the "Tennessee Tease" does not defy gravity by the grace of God alone) elevates one's social status instantly.

3. When long-lost friends and relatives (translation: accidental tourists looking for a free bed and breakfast) arriving from out of town ask where one lives, answer, "right off Old Hickory Boulevard" but never specify which Old Hickory Boulevard. Encompassing the entire perimeter of Nashville, Old Hickory is both the first and last Nashville exit in all four directions. Circling the city a few times while an endless supply of hotel chains beckon usually conveys the obvious.

4. Know the difference between singular (y'all) and plural (all y'alls). Improper use of y'all is the quickest way to catch an overzealous Yankee trying to fit in.

5. That unfortunate "misunderstanding" between the North and South has never been fully resolved. And probably never will be.

In the meantime, if you want a taste of the real (and much cheaper than advertised) Nashville, check out the sites listed below:

Best Barbecue

Served at my house, of course. Next best barbeque can be found at either Bar-B-Cutie or Whitts, depending on your taste preference. Whitts features heaping portions of slow-cooked pork, topped with a mound of slaw and served on a bun with a side of mild, hot or thick rib sauce.

Bar-B-Cutie, a family owned and operated restaurant, serves their hickory-wood smoked pork pretty much the same way, but with a more defined smoky flavor. Both restaurants offer an assortment of side items. Bar-B-Cutie also features an assortment of homemade desserts (fudge pie, key lime pie, banana pudding) for the calorie *un*conscious.

Either restaurant is a great choice, especially on Wednesdays, *aka* bargain day, when barbecue sandwiches are just half price.

Best Authentic Southern Food

If you're looking for authentic Southern food served with an attitude ("eat here or we'll slash the tires on your house"), check out The White Trash Café.

Tasteless and tasty, The White Trash serves up homemade Southern cuisine at its best—and cheapest ("meat and three" for just $6.25—no extra charge for the sociology lesson). Generous portions of greens (turnip, collard, beans), potatoes, fried chicken, Cajun catfish, steaming corn bread, gooey Mississippi Mud pie, and unlimited refills of coma-inducing sweet tea almost make one forget they're paying a surly waitress named Stretch to hurl insults while slinging plates of food.

The White Trash is open Monday-Friday from 10AM-3PM, but if you're not there by noon, mostly everything is sold out (the menu cautions, "when it's gone, it's gone").

If you go, take I-65N to the Wedgewood Avenue exit and turn right, then turn right again at Bransford Avenue and just follow the long line of cars to the tackiest place in town.

Best Field Trip/Historical Site

A category filled with stiff competition—literally—as Nashville is the final resting place of numerous Civil War heroes, ex-presidents (Andrew Jackson, James K. Polk), and music celebrities.

Historical sites such as the Belle Meade Mansion, Carnton Plantation in nearby Franklin, and Sam Davis Home in suburban Smyrna each have their unique charms and characteristics. However, if you have time to visit only one historical site, make it the Hermitage, home of Andrew Jackson ("Old Hickory").

From the moment you set foot onto the 1100+ acres of pristine property (sadly, over 1200 trees were lost in the 1998 tornado), there is a sense of stepping back in time to the mid-19th century when cotton and crinoline reigned supreme.

Almost all of the Greek-Revival style mansion's interior furnishings (including the scenic wallpaper in the entry hall depicting the mythical Telemachus's search for his father, Odysseus) are original. Behind the mansion is the stately tomb of Andrew Jackson and his beloved wife, Rachel.

A nearby museum houses Jackson memorabilia as well as the personal possessions of slaves who lived at the Hermitage.

If you go, take I-40 East to Exit 221A (Old Hickory Blvd.—seriously) and follow the signs. Admission is charged, except on January 8th, when the museum is free for everybody in commemoration of Jackson's decisive victory during the War of 1812 at the Battle of New Orleans.

Best (Cheapest) Lodging

Almost any motel room in Murfreesboro (located thirty minutes southeast of Nashville) costs less than half that of an equivalent room in Nashville. Gas is also cheaper (sometimes as much as twenty cents/gallon) in the 'Boro, but sales tax is horrible everywhere (varies by county, but at least 9.25%).

Best Kept Secret Bargain

The absolute best bargain in Nashville is 200 miles down the road in Tunica, Mississippi, home of more gambling casinos per square mile than Las Vegas.

Although Tennessee prohibits *any* form of gambling, the road to casino perdition starts and finishes right here in Hollywood South.

Every day, buses leave Nashville on both day trips and overnight excursions to various gambling venues in Mississippi and Illinois. Almost all travel packages offer incentives such as free meals and casino coins.

The "Two For One" special, (Tuesdays only), includes transportation to and from Tunica, three buffet meals (featuring traditional Southern and Cajun fare), *and* overnight accommodations at a luxury hotel in Lula (forty minutes down the road from Tunica) for the astonishing price of $18.00 per person. That's right—a mini-getaway to Mississippi for less than twenty dollars.

Of course, they're betting you'll gamble. And most people do. For example, one passenger on a recent excursion complained that he'd lost $300 playing the slots when we stopped for two hours at the Goldstrike Casino to get our "free" buffet lunch.

On the other hand, since I neither drink nor gamble and just bought two postcards (fifty cents apiece), and then interviewed several people for a future article on the lure of casinos, I got off easy. So, if your only agenda is a change of scenery, this deal can't be beat.

There is an almost endless supply of interesting and entertaining sites to visit in and around Nashville. In fact, one of Nashville's most attractive qualities is its central location to just about everything. So y'all come down and visit. And don't forget that hairspray.

—February 23, 2003 *The Tullahoma News*
—March 2, 2003 *The Dispatch*

Author's Note: Sadly, the White Trash Café closed in 2008. It is greatly missed by all.

MEMPHIS ON THE CHEAP: CATFISH, CIVIL RIGHTS AND COTTON COUNTRY

Last month, I began researching inexpensive destinations for our annual family vacation. Surely, there was some bargain basement venue where a writer and her pre-teen daughter could go for some fun and family time. Perhaps even eat food that didn't feature French fries and Styrofoam cups. Sleep soundly. Gain a few collective IQ points. Share a Kodak moment or two. And then return home feeling refreshed and renewed. Not frantically whipping out a credit card to finance snacks at Sonic—after eating our entire travel budget on the first day—would be an added bonus.

Dirt cheap, it turned out, was right down the road on the banks of the muddy Mississippi.

Memphis—home of mouth-watering wood-smoked BBQ and the soothing sound of the blues. Catfish and cotton. Civil rights and wrongs. Giant pandas and small (but well-stocked) independent bookstores (check out Burke's on Poplar Avenue). The famous Sun Studio and a sociology lesson on every corner. Something for everyone on a limited budget.

By using a motel coupon book (available at rest stops along the interstate) and arriving on a Sunday, we found a clean, quiet, no frills motel, conveniently located just fifteen minutes from downtown for under $35.00 a night. The motel was also just ten minutes in the opposite direction from Germantown, an affluent suburb with endless dining choices.

Lunch (BBQ sandwiches piled high with delicious hickory-smoked pork, 'Patriot Fries' and soft drinks) at The Pig On Beale ("pork with an attitude"), and an inexpensive trolley ride around the riverfront started our day on an inexpensive note.

After lunch, shop the schlock shops (endless supply of junk) and peek into the seedy nightclubs (comparatively quiet during the daytime) where B.B. King and other blues artists once plied their craft to huge crowds—there's a lot of history on Beale Street.

The nearby National Civil Rights Museum, formerly known as the Lorraine Motel (where Dr. Martin Luther King, Jr. was assassinated on April 4, 1968) provides a valuable opportunity for visitors to learn more about civil rights, history, and race relations.

The Motel/Museum serves as a historic landmark, memorial, and tribute to a man who craved peace and harmony. It is also the focal point of on-going controversy, as boycotters have posted signs warning the public that the Museum is "exploiting the legacy" of Dr. King by essentially turning the site of his death into a tourist trap.

Regardless of the controversial nature of the landmark, after touring the riveting and disturbing exhibits at the Museum, visitors will have a much better (and more empathic) understanding of the civil rights movement and its impact on all our lives.

Viewing the actual motel room (preserved behind glass in painstaking detail down to the half-finished dinner trays) where Dr. King spent his final hours of life, is an eerie experience that lingers long after leaving the museum.

The legendary Sun Studio (the birthplace of modern rock n' roll) where producer Sam Phillips discovered Elvis, Johnny Cash, Carl Perkins, Jerry Lee Lewis and a zillion other rockabilly types, provides a different "cultural" experience.

For example, the 40-minute Sun tour featured tidbits of quirky music trivia and a chance to try out the actual microphone and vintage sound equipment used by Elvis and others. Rockabilly aficionados may want to bring a camera so an understanding spouse can snap a picture of their 'fifteen minutes' at the microphone.

A visit to the studio gift store (fully stocked with mugs, t-shirts, shot glasses, books, guitar picks, CDs, etc.) and café (sodas and snacks only) rounds out the Sun experience.

After the studio, visit the nearby Memphis Zoo.

The highlight of the zoo experience is absolutely Le Le and Ya Ya, two giant pandas on loan from China. *Caveat:* visiting the cherubic fur balls requires a certain amount of patience and perseverance to navigate the crowds and tight security set up to protect the endangered bears.

And, since Le Le and Ya Ya consume approximately forty pounds of bamboo per day and sleep 12-14 hours per day, the odds of catching them doing anything other than eating or sleeping are not good.

For example, when we arrived, Le Le was blissfully lying on his back, chomping and chewing on his bamboo lunch. Surrounded by a roomful of bamboo, Le Le was in panda paradise—and clearly oblivious to the mesmerized crowd. Still, it's intriguing to see a low-maintenance guy in action.

Before leaving the Panda Pavilion, check out the Bamboo Market, *aka* the panda gift shop (everything from Panda Christmas tree ornaments to Panda tote bags).

Other relatively inexpensive things to do in Memphis: savor real Delta catfish at the Blues City Café, a shabby-chic hole-in-the-wall at 144 Beale Street. Or grab a bag of hot beignets (New Orleans-style donuts rolled in powdered sugar and served hot) at the Beignet Express Café (downtown). Check out the Pink Palace Museum (free on Tuesdays after 1 P.M.). And, if touring Graceland, Elvis' former home and tourist trap extraordinaire, is out of the question, take home at least one token Elvis souvenir for under $3.00 at Elvis Presley's Memphis Store at 126 Beale Street.

—August 31, 2003 *The Huntsville Times*

Author's Note: Prices will, no doubt, have increased since this article was originally published.

IF YOU'VE GOT THE TIME...
THEY'VE GOT THE CRIME

"Some people never go insane...what boring lives they must lead."

Carved on cinderblock years ago by Charles B., a 'guest' of the Turner County jail, the irreverent, but intriguing commentary is one of many (and by far the most tame) pieces of inmate 'art' on display at The Crime and Punishment Museum in Ashburn, Georgia.

The Museum, housed in the former county jail, offers visitors a fascinating (read: morbid) and inexpensive look into the harsh conditions of Southern jails, circa the entire 20th century. Tools of escape (some pretty ingenious devices) and various weapons are on display as are complete menu listings of the "last meals" eaten by condemned men.

A video of the jail's colorful history (it opened in 1907), guided tour of the cells (both men at women occupied space at the jail), and strolling the actual gallows where two men were hanged, round out the unusual museum experience.

Although there is a restaurant (Last Meal Café) located in the museum that serves traditional Southern fare on tin plates and cups, its location directly under the old trap door used for hangings might prove a bit distracting for the squeamish. Besides, until further notice, the café only serves groups of 10 or more with advance reservations.

Thus, it's worth checking out the nearby La Hacienda Mexican Restaurant on Monroe Avenue in Ashburn. Although the restaurant doesn't reach out and grab passersby with great aesthetics, the service is top notch and the food, tasty and very inexpensive.

Even my daughter, a teenager who doesn't like anything, raved about the grilled shrimp quesadilla, stuffed with fresh red and green peppers, onions, and cheese.

After lunch, we headed northwest (State Hwy. 32 to U.S. Hwy. 19 to State Hwy. 49) to Andersonville, the infamous Civil War prison where nearly 13,000 Union prisoners of war died. The national cemetery and former prison grounds are haunting, but inside the nearby visitor center that houses the National Prisoner of War Museum (a memorial to all former American P.O.W.s), an even more disconcerting story unfolds.

Disturbing exhibits, a heartbreaking video presentation featuring family and friends "left behind" when their loved ones were taken prisoner during various recent wars, and memorabilia donated by former P.O.W.s provide a compelling and sobering lesson on the inhumanity of war.

Wait. Wait. And wait some more. That was all that was left to do when sons, husbands, brothers, fathers, and in recent years, daughters, were taken prisoner of war. For those left behind, the wait (and the uncertainty) was the worst, and the anguish could last anywhere from months to years (in one case, eight years and six months).

For those taken captive, in Viet Nam, for example, it was the most horrible endurance test imaginable, e.g., years spent in solitary confinement, crouched, crowded, and shackled in tiny bamboo huts known as "tiger cages." The monotony broken only by beatings and a morning ritual, *bao cao* ("to report"), when a P.O.W. bowed and reported for duty to his captor. An occasional Red Cross package. And an intense will to live—to somehow survive a nightmare that seemingly would never end.

Outside the museum, the serene, pristine grounds hide the horror of a distant time when thousands of men died from disease, overcrowding, and starvation during the last fourteen months of the Civil War. The endless rows of tombstones tell a powerful story of death and despair. Human misery. And the insanity of war.

Down the road, there is a town called Plains that tells a different story…

—April 30, 2004 *The Tullahoma News*

THE PEACEMAKER OF PLAINS

A little over a hundred miles and several light years southwest of Atlanta lies a bucolic hamlet surrounded by pine trees, pecan groves, and peanut farms.

A short row of turn-of-the century buildings including an antique store and trading post along with a modern post office form the downtown. Across the silent railroad tracks and down the road apiece, at the other end of town is a small Baptist church where a humble, faith-driven man is about to begin teaching his Sunday School lesson. That is, as soon as a battery of somber, but stylishly dressed Secret Service agents signal the room is secure.

Welcome to Plains, Georgia, idyllic home of the world's most famous Sunday school teacher, former President Jimmy Carter.

"We had 12,739 visitors last year," confirms Maranatha Baptist Church pastor, Dr. Daniel Ariail. "In addition to our 131 church members." When asked how he copes with the volume, the pastor quips, "blessed are the flexible, for they never get bent out of shape."

Reverend Ariail should know. He wrote the book—actually a 197-page doctoral dissertation—on how to maintain hospitality and normality under arguably bizarre circumstances, namely, armed guards and huge crowds regularly attending Sunday worship service.

"We're a small church with a worldwide outreach," observes Reverend Ariail. He is, of course, referring to the global draw of his most famous, yet eminently accessible congregant, 79-year-old Jimmy Carter, who despite a grueling travel and work schedule, somehow manages to teach Sunday School at the tiny country church 35-40 weeks out of the year.

A few minutes before ten, Jimmy Carter and his ethereal wife, Rosalynn arrive without fanfare, and enter the packed sanctuary via a noisy and frigid waiting room jammed with "overflow" guests seated on metal folding chairs. They—we—will have to settle for hearing the former President deliver his lesson via closed circuit television. Only those who arrive at the crack of dawn have a prayer of being seated in the sanctuary. Aware of this inconvenience, Jimmy Carter lingers behind in the waiting room for almost ten minutes, chatting up the eager audience and even answering a few questions.

Sporting a bolo tie with turquoise accents, dark blue wool jacket and slacks, and spit and polish burgundy loafers, Carter's look and manner are decidedly understated, but quietly charming.

Although the air conditioner has been cranked to Siberian summer so no one nods off during the videotaped service, the aura of the room grows noticeably warmer with the presence of Jimmy Carter. There is something fascinating and yet oddly familiar about this peanut farmer turned President turned peacemaker.

Perhaps it is his altruism-in-action for the poor and disenfranchised. Or his revered title of 'elder statesman'. Or perhaps it's his lifelong record of service to others.

Perhaps it is the magic and mystery of the Deep South and a bygone era that is the real allure—the man and the myth are not easily separated in Dixie. Nor in politics.

Perhaps it's the 'everyman' theme that resonates. If a peanut farmer from the Bible Belt could make it to the Beltway—and back, with his integrity intact, so can anyone in America.

Whatever 'it' is, it keeps people from California to Calcutta and everywhere in between coming in droves to see how a man who once led the free world now leads a humble, but powerfully insightful Sunday School class at Maranatha (the name means "come, Lord) Baptist Church.

Carter begins this particular Sunday's lesson, titled, "The Lord's Supper" with a humorous anecdote about viewing Mel Gibson's *The Passion of the Christ* at a local theater.

"Rosalynn and I went (on a) Tuesday, thinking there wouldn't be a big crowd since it was a weekday…but the Secret Service had to use their influence just to get us two seats together," he said. The crowd laughs at the hominess of it all. Then Carter gets serious and the lesson officially begins.

Mel Gibson did an "outstanding job" in Carter's opinion, of "accurately depicting Scripture." But, adds Carter, "the violence was excessive" and he was "disappointed with the last scene" because he felt the Resurrection was not given its full due, nor was it explained sufficiently enough for non-Christians to understand.

The lesson continues with a mix of personal anecdotes (including a confession that although a born-and-bred Baptist, Carter routinely attended early morning Catholic services during his Navy days because it freed up the rest of the day to spend with his family), references to Scripture, and an interpretive narrative about the symbolism and significance of the Lord's Supper.

All too soon, the lesson concludes and the teacher quietly departs the podium to take his place next to his wife and along with the rest of the congregation, prepares to worship.

Later, offertory plates, hand-crafted from Philippine mahogany by Jimmy Carter (also an accomplished carpenter) and hand-lined with green felt by Rosalynn, are passed around the room. Visitors are politely asked to refrain from tipping the plates upside down to verify the craftsman's initials, J.C., are indeed there.

A little over an hour later, the service concludes with the choir singing, "Christ Receiveth Sinful Men" while the Carters quietly exit the sanctuary.

Once outside, they begin the tedious process of becoming photo ops for the nearly 500 people who have trekked to Plains, endured security checks, and survived the tundra zone just to have their fifteen seconds with a most extraordinary 'ordinary' man.

The Carters' smiles and sincerity remain through every click and flash. Both possess the patience of Job (coincidentally the subject of Reverend Ariail's earlier homily) and the politeness indicative of Southern gentility.

They could be your favorite aunt and uncle, and you could be going over to their house after church for Sunday dinner—but for the fact that as soon as the final snapshot is taken, two men in black hustle the couple into a silver sedan and drive them away. The rest of the Secret Service detail follow close behind in an SUV.

In one surreal moment, the car and its occupants have disappeared down a pastoral country road. The crowd disperses. The church is locked. And life goes back to normal. Except in Plains, where 'normal' seems a little more interesting than usual.

—April 4, 2004 *The Tullahoma News*
—May 1, 2004 *The Huntsville Times*

THE OTHER SIDE OF HIGHWAY 231

What do Martin Luther King, Jr., Jefferson Davis, F. Scott and Zelda Fitzgerald, Hank Williams, Sr. and Rosa Parks all have in common? Turns out, they all spent some of their very interesting lives in Montgomery, Alabama.

Steeped in the legacy of both the Civil War and the Civil Rights movement, Montgomery offers unusual insights into some of the defining moments in our nation's history, a glimpse into the troubled lives of a great literary figure and his passionate, but clearly insane wife (that would be the Fitzgeralds), and a close-up view of how state government works. All for free or very cheap.

At the corner of Madison and Perry Streets in downtown Montgomery stands St. John's Episcopal Church, the oldest Episcopal church in Montgomery. Confederate President Jefferson Davis and his wife worshiped at St. John's during the early days of the War Between the States (as it's known in the Deep South).

The church also hosted the historic Secessionist Convention of Southern Churches in 1861. The pew where the Davis family sat is clearly marked and, along with beautiful stained glass windows (one designed by Louis Tiffany of New York) and elegantly ornate altar, provide visitors a sense of both Southern history and religious tradition.

The church is conveniently located directly across the street from the Guest House International, a quiet, friendly and very modestly priced hotel.

A trolley car stops in front of the hotel and takes riders throughout the downtown "Heritage District," where the majority of Civil War and Civil Rights sites are located.

A tour of the Greek Revival-style State Capitol offers interesting history lessons, but it is just outside the building, in the portico, beneath two tall columns where two divergent worldviews would intersect a century apart.

In February, 1861, Jefferson Davis took the oath of office as President of the Confederate States of America (Montgomery was the provisional capital for three months until the government moved to Richmond) on the steps of the Capitol. The spot in the portico where Davis was inaugurated is marked with a Bronze Star.

A little more than a hundred years later, in March, 1965, Martin Luther King, Jr.'s. historic Selma-to-Montgomery civil rights march ended on the same Capitol steps, just inches from where Jefferson Davis had once sworn to uphold the ideals of the Confederacy.

Two blocks down the street from the Capitol is the Dexter Avenue King Memorial Baptist Church, where Dr. King preached his message of hope and peaceful resistance. Located next door is the Parsonage where Dr. King and his family resided from 1954-1960. Both sites are open to the public (tours are given by appointment and admission is charged).

To the left of the Capitol is the First White House of the Confederacy, built between 1832-1835 by William Sayre, an ancestor of F. Scott Fitzgerald's wife, Zelda Sayre.

The Italianate structure includes a grand dining hall, spacious parlors, a library and seven bedrooms (two downstairs and five upstairs). Period furnishings and many of Davis' personal belongings give the home an air of historical significance as well as a glimpse into nineteenth-century Southern culture. A small gift shop stocks period souvenirs and is staffed by volunteers who gratefully accept donations (admission is free) for the upkeep of the building and relics.

A short trolley ride back toward the Alabama River brings visitors to the Hank Williams, Sr. Museum (the ill-fated country legend died on New Years Day, 1953 at the age of twenty-nine) at 118 Commerce Street.

The museum offers an expansive display of Williams' memorabilia, including his 1952 baby blue Cadillac, and includes an 80-minute video presentation on the life and times of the legendary singer-songwriter. A gift shop is located at the entrance of the museum for those just wanting a postcard or book on the famous musician.

For those looking for a photo-op with the legendary singer, the Hank Williams statue is located a few blocks away at Lister Hill Plaza on North Perry Street.

Just two blocks down the street from the Hank Williams Museum is the Historic Union Station, now the Montgomery Visitor Center. All trolley cars start and finish their downtown routes here.

The impeccably preserved train station provides tourists a comprehensive history of Montgomery, and well-stocked gift shop. Admission is free and includes a short video of things to see and do around Montgomery.

Unfortunately, we ran out of time and didn't get to check out the Rosa Parks Library and Museum at Troy State University's downtown Montgomery campus. The 7,000-square-foot interactive museum features a re-enactment of the 1955 Montgomery Bus Boycott and visitors get to hear actual participants from the Boycott speak. Admission is charged and tours are given by appointment.

Our last stop, before heading further south on Highway 231, was to the F. Scott and Zelda Fitzgerald home at 919 Felder Ave. (not within walking distance of the downtown, nor accessible by trolley) in the artsy (read: upscale) district of Montgomery, near Alabama State University. Admission is free.

The two-story brick home turned museum is a stately memorial to one of the greatest writers of the twentieth century, and his talented, but troubled wife. Scott and Zelda lived together in the house on Felder for only a few months during 1931-1932, but if those walls could talk…

And in a sense, they do—the extensive collection of letters that passed between Scott and Zelda, the personal items that defined their taste and talent, prints of Zelda's paintings (no amateur, her work was widely shown) and a haunting portrait of a woman chased and eventually caught by the demons of schizophrenia—tell the painful story of two lives defined by madness and brilliance.

Strolling the peaceful grounds, one can imagine the ideas flowing for Scott's classic love story-in-progress, *Tender Is The Night*, which, partially because of Zelda's breakdown in January, 1932, wasn't finished until 1934.

Neither the huge shade trees nor the calming gardens could provide Zelda either sanctuary or sanity, so, by early 1932, Scott had to place Zelda in a Baltimore clinic.

In 1940, at the age of 44, Scott suffered a fatal heart attack. Eight years later, Zelda, then institutionalized in an Asheville, North Carolina sanitarium, died in a fire that swept through the facility one March evening. They left behind one daughter, Scottie, a legacy of great literature (Zelda's novel, *Save Me the Waltz*, has a distinct voice with unforgettable passages), and some memorable moments in Montgomery which have been preserved in the world's only museum dedicated to the Fitzgeralds.

Montgomery proved to be a rare serendipitous experience on the long road to Panama City, Florida, which in turn proved entirely predictable—a tourist trap of grand proportion with all the usual suspects: overpriced motels, huge crowds at the beach, sand, sun, and seaweed (listed in reverse order of occurrence), traffic jams, and okay, great seafood (the smoked tuna pate at Calypso's in Panama City Beach was exceptional).

Gulf World, a marine park (complete with a parrot show featuring the exotic birds answering addition and subtraction problems with disturbing accuracy and dolphins performing acrobatics to the tune of Rock classics) located in Panama City Beach, is one of the few sources of cerebral stimulation to be found in the vicinity—thus, well worth the exorbitant price of admission.

An afternoon at the city beach and strolling through a few beachside schlock shops rounded out our brief, but costly Florida experience, or as my disgruntled thirteen-year-old daughter put it, "our visit to the dark side of the Sunshine State."

Travel *caveat*: enjoy your Dixie cup of free orange juice offered at the Florida Welcome Center—it is the first, last and only thing that's free on the other side of Highway 231.

—August 29, 2004 *The Tullahoma News*

BARDSTOWN, KENTUCKY: BOURBON CAPITAL OF AMERICA AND MUCH MORE....

Kentucky is the South's best kept secret. Surrounded by seven states and situated squarely on the way to its distinctively different neighbors, Kentucky is easy to miss and dismiss.

A quick stopover on the way to somewhere else, perhaps north to the Land of Lincoln or south to the 'real' Dixie. An afterthought (what is the capital of Kentucky, anyway?). A border state that couldn't make up its mind during the Civil War. Kentucky may be all these things, but it is also a friendly place filled with hidden treasures. Most of which are free or very inexpensive.

For example, just a few hours north of Nashville is a quaint little burg called Bardstown, *aka* the Bourbon Capital of America. Surrounded by three large, working distilleries (Maker's Mark, Heaven Hill, and Jim Beam), Bardstown offers visitors a crash course in the methods and madness of moonshine as well as important history lessons (just down the road is Hodgenville, birthplace of Abraham Lincoln), entertainment (site of the famous outdoor musical, *The Stephen Foster Story*), and pastoral scenery in the woods and rolling hills of Kentucky's heartland.

All three distilleries provide free tours of their facilities and each has a gift shop stocked with such necessities as Jim Beam wearing apparel and gourmet bourbon chocolates (*caveat*: not your father's Hershey bar, this candy packs a real punch, especially for nondrinkers). And yes, there are plenty of free samples.

At the Jim Beam Distillery, visitors are also invited to view a film, *America's First Family of Bourbon*, which chronicles the 209-year history of the Beam family business and then tour the nearby Beam House, built in 1911. Listed in the National Register of Historic Places, the elegant two-story house was once the home of T. Jeremiah Beam, son of Jim Beam.

Rare family photographs and heirlooms scattered throughout the house recall a bygone era of glitz and glamour. In the tasting parlor, visitors can sample various bourbons (in addition to its flagship bourbon, Jim Beam manufactures four other 'small batch' premium bourbons, each with their own distinctive flavor) every day but Sunday.

After sampling free bourbon and bonbons, visitors can learn about the spirited history of Bardstown by touring the Oscar Getz Museum of Whiskey History & Bardstown Historical Museum, located in Spalding Hall, adjacent to St. Joseph's Proto-Cathedral. A Proto-Cathedral is the first of its kind, in this case, the first Catholic cathedral built west of the Allegheny Mountains, way before the Catholic Archdiocese relocated to Louisville.

The cathedral, a historic landmark in its own right built 1816-1819, houses many spectacular paintings and altar adornments donated by Francis I, King of the Two Sicilies, and Pope Leo XII. Worship services are still conducted on Saturday evenings and Sunday mornings and church tours are available.

The Getz Museum, used as a hospital to treat both Union and Confederate soldiers during the Civil War, now contains countless vintage whiskey bottles (remember, this is the bourbon capital of America), tools, clothing, documents, and artifacts that tell the story of how the whiskey industry evolved in Bardstown.

It is a story of bold personalities, friendly geography and impeccable timing that ignited an American tradition. Pioneers Jacob Beam, William Heavenhill, and Robert Samuels came west to Kentucky in search of a better life. What they found was a goldmine—limestone spring water essential for mellow-flavored whiskey, abundant land to grow the basic ingredients of whiskey (e.g., corn, barley, and rye), and a young nation of rebels looking for a new "official drink" (rum was the favored drink of the British, and very unpopular after the Revolutionary War).

Other nearby museums include The Civil War Museum, The Women's Civil War Museum, the Wildlife & Natural History Museum. All are located just off the square in downtown Bardstown.

Across from the square is the Talbott Tavern, the oldest western stagecoach stop in America. The Talbott Tavern still serves meals (Kentucky favorites like fried chicken and chess pie are de rigueur) and provides moderately priced lodging for travelers wanting to sleep in the same rooms that colorful characters such as Jesse James and General George Patton once occupied.

If your lodging taste leans more toward criminal chic, check out the Jailer's Inn Bed & Breakfast in the center of Bardstown. Formerly known as the Nelson County Jail, the B&B is located in the renovated front jail, originally built in 1819. The back jail, built in 1874, remains unchanged and was in operation for its intended purpose until 1987, making it the oldest jail in the state. Tours are available. Orange jumpsuits optional.

For those just looking for a bed and blanket in a quiet, clean room, head to the Bardstown Inn, directly across from My Old Kentucky Home State Park on Stephen Foster Avenue. The manager, a New Jersey transplant named Mark, will even keep the pool open late so your disgruntled teenagers can swim a few extra laps.

Dining choices in Bardstown abound. Locals raved about Kreso's, a Bosnian family-owned restaurant located downtown, just north of the square. Others swore by both Asian Garden, an inexpensive and expansive buffet-style restaurant, and Xavier's, an upscale bistro located in the basement of the Getz Museum. We finally chose Los Nopales, a Mexican restaurant on the outskirts of town, where we filled up on free chips and salsa, and then dined on tacos and sodas for less than twenty dollars.

Although Bardstown has more than enough attractions to keep visitors occupied for days on end, the Fort Knox Depository, containing an impressive $100 billion in gold bullion, beckons from behind its mysterious and heavily guarded building just off Highway 31W, twenty minutes northwest of Bardstown. No visitors are allowed, so bring a telephoto lens to snap a photo of the richest half-acre in the world.

Visitors are welcome at the nearby Patton Museum of Cavalry and Armor, also located at Fort Knox, a working military installation. Dedicated to the memory of World War II hero General George S. Patton, the museum features an extensive collection of Patton's personal effects as well as military equipment that originally belonged to him. Other exhibits on the rotating display include armor weapons and machinery depicting the use of cavalry and armor from WWI to the 1978 prototype of the M1 Abrams Tank.

Back in Bardstown, things are quiet. For now. The critically-acclaimed outdoor musical, *The Stephen Foster Story*, which runs from June-August and draws thousands of visitors from across the country has shut down for the season. Composer Stephen Foster wrote "My Old Kentucky Home" in 1818, after visiting Federal Hill (now My Old Kentucky Home State Park) and for the past 46 years, Bardstown has hosted the popular musical.

Autumn will soon arrive in Bardstown. And with it, numerous special events. Breathtaking foliage. Plenty of bourbon and bluegrass. And quiet memories waiting to be made in a state that shouldn't be overlooked.

By the way, Frankfort is the capital of Kentucky.

—October 10, 2004 *The Huntsville Times*
—November 26, 2004 *The Tullahoma News*

HOT DEALS ON COOL VENUES

Your tax refund is a distant memory. Your raise did not materialize. Gas prices hover around $2.00 a gallon. And now, the kids are out of school getting on your last nerve.

You want out—*Lost* is not just your favorite television show—it's your dream.

Well, I can't get you to Hawaii on a dime (although I once got myself there on little more than a whim and a good sales pitch), but there are a few quirky places right down the road almost as remote from the modern world as the survivors of Oceanic Flight 815 are—without the annoying polar bear to chase you off. Even better, the price is right—free to very cheap. All you'll need is gas money (okay, that's the bad news), a few dollars for admission to the sites, lunch money, and a willingness to take a walk on the mild side (translation: kids may moan and groan).

The Ave Maria Grotto in Cullman, Alabama (just 50 miles south of Huntsville), offers an intriguing look into one man's lifelong pursuit of perfection in detail.

Brother Joseph Zoettl, a Benedictine monk, arrived in Cullman from Bavaria in 1892 and soon developed a hobby—building miniature shrines from stone, concrete, and 'junk' sent to him from all over the world. By the time he died in 1961, Brother Zoettl had handcrafted, with painstaking detail, 125+ miniature replicas of world famous shrines (including the Basilica in Lourdes, which he completed at age 80), creating a three-acre forested fairyland in the heart of Dixie.

The tireless artisan's work (made even more impressive by the fact that Brother Zoettl never let his handicap—a severe hunchback resulting from a accident early in life—affect his passion for perfection) can be seen on the grounds of the Benedictine Abbey. Catholic visitors should check out the well-stocked gift shop adjacent to the Grotto.

If you're looking for a more militaristic example of passion and perseverance, head northeast to Middlesboro, Kentucky by way of

Harrogate, Tennessee, home of the renowned Abraham Lincoln Museum (located on the campus of Lincoln University).

The museum, originally built as a tribute to East Tennesseans who remained loyal to Lincoln during the Civil War, houses one of the most complete Lincoln collections in the country, including over 20,000 books, photos, sculptures, and manuscripts that tell the story of great turmoil during the Lincoln years. Admission is charged, but reduced rates are available for seniors and children under twelve.

While Lincoln presided over one of the most divisive times in our nation's history, World War II united Americans in a way that has yet to be seen again. And it is from WWII that our next venue originates.

Glacier Girl, a completely restored P-38 warplane, resides at the Lost Squadron Museum in Middlesboro, Kentucky, just minutes across the scenic Cumberland Gap from the Lincoln Museum. She is a testimonial to the perseverance and huge financial backing of retired entrepreneur and military man J. Roy Shoffner.

The P-38 fighter plane, along with five other P-38s and two B-17 bombers were on their way to England in 1942 when they ran into bad weather and eventually crash-landed on an icecap in Greenland.

Although all the men of what became known as the "Lost Squadron" survived their ordeal and were eventually rescued, the planes were left behind.

Over the years, twelve expeditions would fail to recover the planes, buried in snow (35-50 feet per year) and ice.

But then came J. Roy Shoffner and his dream to bring home and restore at least one of the ill-fated P-38s. And bring it home he did—after fifty years and digging through 268 feet of ice, his team, led by Bob Cardin (who now manages the museum), finally brought the plane affectionately named Glacier Girl home and after another ten years, completely restored the plane, which in 2002, once again took flight after sixty years of being 'grounded.'

Admission to the museum is free, but donations are appreciated. Glacier Girl was not a cheap date—Shoffner has spent over four million dollars on her.

Before you leave the area, check out the Cumberland Gap Visitor's Center—it's free and offers a film presentation on Daniel

Boone country as well as an assortment of interesting exhibits showcasing the "Gateway to the West."

While you're in the neighborhood (okay, it's about another 100 miles), head west to the Shaker Village, one of 24 Shaker communities established in the U.S. during the 19th century, in South Union, Kentucky (just outside Bowling Green).

The Shakers, a much-maligned religious sect that believe poverty, celibacy and orderliness are the path to enlightenment, are now down to four actual members living in Maine. Still, the Shaker Village Museum in South Union has managed to preserve a unique way of life so visitors can learn firsthand about the quirky, but devoted Shakers who once inhabited the region.

The Shakers left Kentucky almost 100 years ago, but their legacy remains in both their craftsmanship (now recreated by local artisans) and unparalleled commitment to their beliefs. A two-room gift shop provides visitors the opportunity to sample Shaker foods (the herbs are shipped in from Maine), books, and furniture.

The Shaker Tavern, circa 1869, a nearby bed and breakfast, offers reasonably priced accommodations.

After leaving Shaker country, head across U.S. Highway 68 toward Russellville and check out Roy's Pit Bar-B-Q for lunch—just about everything on the menu is under $5.00, but tastes like it should cost a lot more.

About twenty minutes west of Russellville is the world's fourth tallest monument—the Jefferson Davis Memorial. You can't miss it. Completely renovated and open to the public again, the memorial offers a startling contrast to the pastoral landscape—and a reminder that things weren't always so quiet in the South.

Last stop on the nickel (well, five dollar) tour—Schlabach's Bakery in Guthrie, Kentucky. The aroma of homemade breads, rolls, pies, cakes, and cookies at the Amish bakery will beckon long before you turn off U.S. Highway 68 onto Highway 181 (slow down, horse-drawn buggies appear out of nowhere with alarming regularity) and head south toward Guthrie.

The bakery is open 8 AM to 5 PM, Monday through Wednesday, Friday and Saturday. They're closed on Thursday, Sunday and the month of January. Call ahead and reserve numerous loaves of the best homemade bread you've tasted since Granny kneaded the dough herself. And don't forget the mule ear (molasses) cookies and hot cinnamon rolls. For more information, call: 1-270-265-3459. Sorry, there's no website. The Amish believe in virtue, not virtual reality.

After bagging your stash of sweets, head to nearby I-24, head south toward Nashville and resume life in the fast lane. Until the next time, when you're ready to get 'lost' again.

—July 3, 2005 *The Huntsville Times*
Author's Note: Glacier Girl has moved on since this article first appeared and is no longer in Kentucky. Schlabach's bakery, on the other hand, is still open for business and as delicious as ever. But still no website...

WE'LL ALWAYS HAVE PARIS…
AND MUCH MORE

Okay, so it's not that Paris… but Paris, Tennessee does have its charms, namely its gateway location to other endearing and eccentric spots located in the northwest corner of our state. And did I mention a great Christmas card photo-op lurks right in the middle of Paris—a 60-foot replica of the famed Eiffel Tower.

Originally constructed in 1990 from 500 pieces of Douglas Fir and 6,000 steel rods by engineers at Christian University in Memphis, the scale model Tower now stands at the entrance of Memorial Park, a tribute to the city's namesake (in honor of the Marquis de Lafayette, a Parisian aristocrat who fought in both the American and French Revolutions).

Located about two hours northwest of Nashville, there are two other stops of interest along the way.

First, lunch. Check out Mazatlan Mexican Restaurant in Waverly, just off U.S. Highway 70 about an hour west of Nashville.

Both times we've eaten there, the food has been tasty (complimentary salsa is spicy enough to open up sinuses), the service great, and best of all, costs under $20 to feed a family of three (including soft drinks).

Next, follow Highway 70 over to Camden and check out the only freshwater pearl farm and museum in the United States. Tours are available for groups of 15 or more, and advance reservations are required (although individuals can tag along with a group). The full tour includes a visit to the pearl farm to observe the culturing techniques used by local divers, a biology lesson on mollusks (that's where pearls come from), an overview of the area's musseling industry and a demonstrative narration of Tennessee's official gem and its history. A full-catered lunch is also provided.

For those on a tight budget, there is the free walk-in version, which includes a video clip on the history of pearls and tour of the museum (featuring various articles and exhibits explaining freshwater pearl-culturing and implanting techniques as well as samples of the exotic gem that's grown in the nearby Tennessee River). The adjacent jewelry showroom provides ample temptation to indulge oneself with a bauble—so, unless you have stoic resolve, bring a credit card—this is not Stuckey's schlock shop.

If you're ready to call it a day, the nearby Birdsong Resort offers reasonably priced accommodations in a pastoral setting.

After leaving Paris, head west to Kenton, home of both the rare white squirrel and a very nice man named L.A. Baucom, who graciously welcomes visitors from all over the world into his back yard to view the exotic rodents scampering among the tree tops of the giant willow oaks and magnolias that canopy his back yard.

Baucom is admittedly nutty about squirrels and his tender devotion to these vulnerable creatures that many see as mere backyard nuisances is especially impressive in an age of indifference.

Cedar squirrel houses and bedding boxes, pecans shipped up from Georgia, and plenty of tender loving care can be found at Baucom's residence on Poplar Street (Baucom even graciously supplies insect repellant to combat the nasty mosquitoes that torment guests hoping to catch a glimpse of the elusive albino squirrels whose ancestors first came to Kenton in 1888). The retired grocer will even give you a bucket of pecans and instructions on calling them down from the trees (it works, but as soon as they see you're not him, the mischievous squirrels dart back up the trees—only Baucom can hand feed them).

Between Baucom's unwavering commitment and the financial contribution of Kenton businessman Tom Wade who has purchased large quantities of wood for housing and supplies free grain to anyone who asks to feed the critters, the approximately fifty remaining albino squirrels that have survived such hardship as disease, merciless eighteen-wheelers, and starvation (last year, too much rainfall washed pollen off the walnut and pecan trees, resulting in a severe shortage of nuts), now have a fighting chance of survival.

After leaving Kenton, head down U.S. Highway 45 to Trenton and check out the world's largest *veilleuses-theieres* (night light teapots) collection.

The collection of rare porcelain teapots are on display 24 hours a day at Trenton's City Hall (visitors have to go through the police department after hours). Admission is free.

All 525 veilleuses, once the personal property of Dr. Frederick Freed, a Trenton physician who traveled extensively, were donated to the city in 1955.

The collection, a lifelong hobby of Freed's includes pieces from Russia, Egypt, Turkey, and Switzerland. Four of the teapots originally belonged to Napoleon's family and the entire collection is valued at $8-10 million. All are unique pieces of art dating from 1750-1860.

Next door to the teapot museum is Rosedale Manor, circa 1868. The charming two-story bed & breakfast, partially hidden behind a curtain of huge magnolias and a lush garden covered with roses and azaleas beckons visitors to a quieter era.

Last stop before leaving the area—the Davy Crockett museum. The famous frontiersman ("y'all can go to hell, I'm going to Texas") died in 1836 defending the Alamo. His last home in Tennessee was a log cabin in the tiny town of Rutherford and is now a museum open to the public Memorial Day thru Labor Day (other times by appointment). The grave of Rebecca Hawkins Crockett (Davy's mother) is located next to the cabin. Admission is charged.

Perhaps not as sophisticated as its European counterpart, Paris, Tennessee and the small communities to the northwest of our state still provide many opportunities for an interesting, memorable, and eminently affordable getaway. Bon voyage...

—October 23, 2005 *The Huntsville Times*

THE SPY WHO LOVED ANNISTON

By all accounts, Colonel Farley Berman was a character straight out of *Casablanca*, a spy who loved intrigue, adventure, and, as it turns out, Anniston, Alabama.

Berman, an Alabama native, enlisted in the service during WWII and spent most of his career in Foreign Intelligence. The spy from Anniston was originally stationed in North Africa, along the Barbary Coast—an exotic venue ripe with espionage, shady deals and lifelong romance—Berman met his wife Germaine while on the job.

Spying on each other (she was with the French Resistance), Farley and Germaine were a perfect match. In addition to a shared career, the Farleys loved to travel and collect historical artifacts. And eventually, the spies who used up four passports each, settled down in Anniston and founded the Berman Museum of World History.

The museum features five distinct galleries including The Deadly Beauty exhibit, a tribute to the longevity and deadliness of the spy business (tools of the trade date back to the sixteenth-century and were just as fatal as today's high tech weapons). From classy (a silver flute that fires a .22 caliber bullet when the right note is hit) to clever (a box of throat lozenges that conceals a tiny pistol in the box) to conspicuous (a royal Persian scimitar encrusted with close to 1,300 diamonds and rubies, accented with a 10-carat emerald set in gold), each piece tells a tale of timeless intrigue.

Artifacts (including Hitler's silver tea service which probably made its way out of Germany in somebody's bedroll) and various weapons from WWI and WWII (including a German bend barrel gun that could fire accurately around corners) are featured in another gallery.

Strolling through the Guns of War exhibit is a bit disturbing—as the timeline moves toward the present, the weapons grow larger, more deadly and less forgiving. Size, it seems does matter. And skill. But most of all, survival.

"It is well that war is so terrible, else men would learn to love it too much," Robert E. Lee once cautioned. History, it seems, is at odds with the General's wisdom.

For those whose taste lean toward the aesthetic and exotic, the Shared Treasures Exhibit features an extensive collection of both sacred and secular works of Asian art dating back to the Xia Dynasty (2205-1806 B.C.) in China and the Edo Period in Japan (1603 A.D.-1868 A.D.).

The exhibit, now a permanent part of the Berman Museum, was donated by Dr. and Mrs. Oliver Foo, retired educators who live in Anniston. The Foos, originally from Taiwan, collected Asian Art for decades, including burial shrines, vases, Chinese cloisonné, and 16th century blue and white export porcelain.

Captivated by cowboys? The American West Gallery offers a look back at the wild and wooly days of saloon girls, gunfights, and gold. And since life in the glory days of westward expansion often ended at the point of a gun, there is also a weapons display featuring the most respected names in the West: Colt, Remington, and Wesson. For Civil War aficionados, the display also includes the traveling pistols of Confederate President Jefferson Davis.

While in the neighborhood, check out the Anniston Museum of Natural History (affiliated with the Smithsonian) right next door.

The tropical garden area located at the entrance of the Anniston Museum is both exotic and picture postcard perfect. Inside, exhibits include Sand to Cedars (showcasing the biodiversity of Alabama), Attack and Defense (survival of the fittest—not for the squeamish), Designs for Living (a huge ornithology collection—over 400 species of birds), and Ancient Egypt (2,300-year-old mummies are the guests of honor).

The Anniston Museum also has a gift shop with a decent assortment of reasonably priced mementoes.

No trip to Anniston is complete until you've tried an oatmeal-macaroon-chocolate chip-and nut cookie from Aliza's. It's simply the best cookie in the South (okay, taste is subjective, but if this cookie connoisseur tells you it's good, believe it).

Based in Anniston, Aliza's Cookies come in a variety of tasty flavors including lemon crisp with white chocolate, Caribbean jammers (a macaroon and almond concoction), key lime kreme and double chocolate chip. Currently, Aliza's cookies are available only by mail order (free samples were doled out at the Alabama Welcome Center last summer and I was immediately hooked).

Numerous nearby fast food restaurants, relatively (emphasis on relatively) cheap gas, and inexpensive lodging make Anniston an economical weekend destination. And because of a spy who loved Alabama, an intriguing history lesson.

—July 11, 2006 *The Tullahoma News*

PART FIVE
THE LONG GOODBYE:
My Mother, Myself

IN THE COMPANY OF BAD DAUGHTERS

Bad daughter. That's me.

I live nearly 700 miles away from my elderly, disabled mother.

I do not phone daily. Nor do I underwrite the considerable medical, household, and personal costs that allow my mother to stay in the house she bought and paid for long before most women were employed, much less homeowners.

And now, I've committed the ultimate sin against parents. I'm not coming home for the holidays. Worse, I am cursed with an increasingly rare condition: honesty.

While mom's cronies congratulate her on her determination to stay put, I have the audacity to ask what, if anything, is accomplished by living alone in chronic poverty, shut off from the rest of the world. Just to make a point. And the point is?

Independence. The most valued commodity (and formidable obstacle) of old age. Lose it and die. It's that simple.

Independence, or the illusion of, is what keeps rarely driven, but perfectly maintained automobiles sitting in garages all across America. Including my mom's. Tuned up, oil freshly changed, and rarin' to go. An average of nine miles a year. Not nearly far enough from the pain and problems of old age.

Independence, or the potential loss of, is the leading cause of heart palpitations among the elderly in the waiting line at the dreaded driver's license station. Denying an elderly person their driver's license is the equivalent of rescinding their license to live.

Independence is also commonly mistaken for paranoia. For example, inability to read one's phone bill (who can?) leads to theories about price fixing (most paranoia is grounded in reality). Bar codes are also part of the pricing conspiracy (so far, everything tracks). And don't even mention the world wide web. It's a guaranteed lecture on the New World Order and rumors about those elusive black helicopters.

Independence is what causes the rest of the world to suddenly 'mumble' when they should be speaking clearly. And, it is what makes being a 'good daughter' next to impossible.

I should know.

So, for all the other bad daughters out there, I offer the following advice:

- Realize that you are no match for independence. It is bigger than you. Hey, it's bigger than your parent(s). That's why they won't give it up. Control freaks to the end.

- Face the fact that you're completely alone when it comes to dealing with your parent's need for independence (read: stubbornness). Spouses, routinely reduced to prepubescent wimps in less time than it takes to shake a cane, are no match for your parents. Your kids, parasites in their own right, offer little solace. "When grandpa dies, do we get his money?" Friends stare blankly. Their parents are doing fine, thank you. Or they lucked out and were born orphans.

- Agencies for the elderly, usually run by idealistic bureaucrats barely old enough to vote, are largely out of touch with the needs of anyone born before the dawn of cyberspace. "So, why aren't these elderly folks, like, on the Net? Then they wouldn't be, like, so lonely." Duh. Like most Washington-based bureaucracies, the Department of Aging is no more than a paper mill designed on a grand scale by other bad sons and daughters who happened to get elected to Congress. Their gain. Our pain. The Washington Way.

- Doctors are not your friend. Anybody who prescribes medication that is both prohibitively expensive and requires reading instructions that span three or more typewritten pages is obviously trying to reduce their caseload of elderly patients.

Chances are, mom will be dead before she makes her way through the dissertation-length directions. Or, if she has to spend the grocery money on medications, she'll probably starve. It's managed care, the next generation. But hey, at least the white coats are good for a trial size Prozac. Not that you have anything to be depressed about…which leads to my final piece of advice: You can't afford to cry, so you absolutely must laugh. It's a matter of survival. Yours.

Finally, and most importantly, avoid at all cost, 'good daughters.' You know the type. Stable. Reliable. Would never consider living more than three blocks from home. Considers a social life frivolous. Wears sensible shoes and radiating halo.

Self-imposed martyrdom is an impossible act to follow. But so is independence. Maybe that's why there are so many bad daughters.

—November 28, 1997 *The Dispatch*

THE BEGINNING OF THE END

(Part One of Five Part Series)

S he came here to die, she told me. I believe her. That's just like my mother. Inconvenient to the end.

How she got here, I do not know. Sheer willpower, I guess. After all, this is the same woman who has survived an assortment of tragedies large and small (including a columnist daughter who writes about them) that would leave the hardiest person contemplating a trip to the garage. Close door. Turn on motor. Turn off pain.

Not my mother. Every crisis—every tragedy—makes her more determined to survive. Even if it kills me.

"Grandma looks really bad," observes my daughter, Nova, as we roll to a stop in front of the TWA terminal at the Nashville International Airport. I am oblivious. All I know is that I'm characteristically late. Off to a bad start. Bad daughter to the end.

Jumping out of the car, I quickly grab my mother's three bags, toss them into the car and roll her wheelchair up to the passenger side of my car. Putting the brake on the wheelchair, I wait for her to stand up and lower herself into the car. She doesn't move. She's ticked off at me for being late. It's going to be a long week. Suddenly, a baggage clerk appears and before I know it, lifts her into the car.

Without a word, we're on our way to the interstate. It's the tail end of rush hour. "I'll stop at the mall and we'll get something to eat." A peace offering for my tardiness.

She sits quietly. Chalk white. But, like a self-absorbed 12-year-old, I am more preoccupied with what my punishment is going to be for my tardiness.

She eats very little. And drinks less. And then she asks to leave. A clue the size of Texas.

Something is wrong. Very wrong. My mother asking to leave the mall. No way.

She needs help getting to the bathroom. And into bed. She hates to ask, she says. But just this once...

Truthfully, it's not "just this once." It has been often in the last year. And we have talked about it. At least I had. And she had listened. Occasionally. The dreaded "talk." The evil 'n' word. Nursing home.

Resistance. Denial. Futility. "I'd rather be dead," she'd say with absolute finality. And I'd rather be dead than have this discussion again.

So we don't talk about it anymore. I lift. Watch somewhat helplessly. Grow sad. And grieve for a loss that's coming. Sooner, rather than later.

The following day, she sleeps most of the afternoon away on the patio. Previews of coming attractions. Sleeping more than awake. A dress rehearsal for death. Soon, I'll be an orphan. Officially alone. My new and unimproved reality.

My reverie is broken by the faint sound of her stirring. "Could you take me to the hospital now?" she asks. Very polite.

The strangeness of the situation increases exponentially. My mother would rather reveal her true age than voluntarily check into a hospital. This is bad, I suddenly realize. Very bad.

Tests are run. Indignities, large and small, are withstood. The doctor appears, disappears, and reappears. A nurse asks me to help. They are short-handed, she explains apologetically. I lift, pull, tug, roll my mother. More tests. She endures it all quietly.

An I.V. drips fluids into her dehydrated body. She has a fever, they say. No blankets. Instead, she must tough out the chills until a diagnosis tells them what to do. She doesn't complain. She's a professional patient. Polio did that for her. Or to her.

The test results reveal a severe kidney infection. "If you hadn't brought her in when you did, she would have died," the doctor tells me matter-of-factly. "Her age, poor general health, history—why is she living alone?" I know that look. Bad daughter.

I forgive him. Obviously the offspring of healthy parents, he does not know the complexity of dealing with physically frail parents who eat their emotionally fragile adult children for breakfast.

A second I.V. drips a powerful new antibiotic into her bloodstream that will attack this latest threat to her life.

She comes home with me later that night. Weak. Frail. Exhausted. Sleep will come easy for her.

Not me. Major decisions have to be made. Sooner rather than later. Adulthood paging Shalynn.

Ready or not...

—May 29, 1999 *The Dispatch*

REALITY PAGING DEADBEAT DAUGHTER

(Part Two of Five Part Series)

"Hello, I'm the deadbeat daughter that lives 700 miles away from her frail, aged, and now very ill mother. You've probably heard about me (God knows what you've heard). Anyway, would you be willing to pitch in and help me, sans compensation (deadbeat daughter is also flat broke), so my mother can return home to recuperate?"

While scanning the list of names—a mix of friends and strangers (to me)—my mother had finally revealed "might help" during her recuperation, I rehearse my dramatic opening lines.

Lose the deadbeat daughter, I tell myself. I'm doing the best I can.

Sure, good daughters live across the street from their aged parents, are always available at a moment's notice, and never become freelance writers that wander the country in search of their next story. Which as it turns out, is playing out right under my own roof...

I pick up the phone and place my first call. I introduce myself and briefly relay the sequence of events: My mother has been very ill. She'll need someone to check on her every day after she returns home. It's important that she eats regularly, takes her medication, and stays hydrated. Maintenance stuff. Not skilled care. Just a babysitter, of sorts.

Until I can get to Moline next month. I have responsibilities, I explain. I homeschool my eight-year-old daughter. And then there's my part-time writing/publicist career.

Yes, I homeschool my daughter. Yes, I'm engaged to the author I work for. And yes, our work is somewhat portable. But we have field trips scheduled, achievement testing, a recital—commitments to fulfill.

Yes, I could drop everything. Deadbeat mother. One step below deadbeat daughter. And another generation does their time on the couch...

Two more phone calls. Three days covered, four to go. "Why can't your mother just stay at your house?" asks a voice at the other end of the line.

My house is completely handicap inaccessible. I live in the middle of nowhere. I have to travel for my work. I don't feel comfortable leaving my eight-year-old to supervise my elderly mother (although I have done so several times). I can't stay in my house 24-hours-a-day. Take your pick.

I know. Lame excuses. But I did consider it. And decided that mom would be better off in her own home. It's small, accessible, and centrally located. Help is only minutes away. Familiar and manageable surroundings.

Friends to help. Professionals to provide ancillary services. And time to recuperate. In a logical universe, my plan made sense. Unfortunately, we do not live in a logical—or forgiving—universe. But I'm getting ahead of myself...

Three more phone calls. All seven days of the week for the next three weeks are finally covered. I am pleased with myself. Next, social service agencies. First, Meals-On-Wheels. I request immediate delivery.

They'll try, promises Donna, the Meals-On-Wheels coordinator. She explains, "Nobody wants to volunteer anymore." They're very short on help. I tell her that my daughter delivered Meals-On-Wheels for a year when she was in first grade. "And later won a national award for community service." Maternal pride. She is astonished. A child doing volunteer work.

I am astonished. Adults *not* doing volunteer work. Maybe it's because they don't know, I offer.

"They know—we've placed paid ads in the local newspapers, even offered to pay mileage...still nobody comes." She sounds beleaguered.

"Well," I persist, "my readers don't know." So I'll tell them. And they'll come...

So, if you're reading this and have even a remote need to do a good deed, delivering Meals-On-Wheels is a much needed service and with so many routes available, chances are there's one in a neighborhood near you.

And hey, like any relationship, it's not a lifetime commitment. Do it for a month. Or two. Do it for the summer with your kids. Just do it. Please. And watch yourself grow. In all the ways that matter most.

Now back to my mother. And more long distance phone calls. Visiting Nurses. Social workers. And home health aides. It's a snap. Almost too easy. I'm feeling confident. Smug. And relieved.

My tour of duty is almost over. She will go home and recuperate. I will get my life back. So I thought…

—June 4, 1999 *The Dispatch*

THE LONG GOODBYE

(Part Three of Five Part Series)

"This is absolutely the last year I'm doing this, Mom."

She is taller than she was yesterday. I'm certain of it. But that look...vintage indignation. Hands on hips. Eye contact. An authoritative tone of voice. Where did all that come from? When did that special brand of parental hell known as pre-adolescence creep up on me?

"Did you hear me?" she persists. "Look at all these babies..." She makes a sweeping gesture toward the numerous babystrollers lined up to see the mall Easter Bunny.

Cherubic babies. Tantrumming toddlers. Sleepy preschoolers. But no indignant pre-pubescent children. Except mine.

It's been a tradition since 1980 when I first stood in Bunny line at the mall with my cousin's infant daughter. Now a sophomore in college, her days of crinoline and candy are long gone. Her younger sister bought me a few more years of bunny visits. And then came my daughter, Nova.

Nine more Easters have passed and I'm still trying to stop something that can't be stopped. Time.

We inch toward the giant bunny. "Do you see his wire screen mouth?" demands Nova. "He's a regular person pretending to be a bunny. *Duh.*" Taller and jaded.

I smile my sincerest "mommie dearest" smile through clenched teeth. "Well, you're still going to sit on his lap and I'm still going to take your picture, and if you behave, I'll buy you a Happy Meal."

"A Happy Meal?" She brightens up. "And the blue metallic nail polish at Claire's." Oblivious to the incongruity of her desires, she extends her small hand to seal the deal.

Happy Meals and hairspray. Boys and Barbies. Secret longings for an Elmo doll. Fan mail. Email. Animorphs. Nickelodeon and *Newsweek* (she reads it cover to cover). Cellular phones and cartoons. And did I mention clothes?

"First graders are cute, third graders are cool," explains Nova with more than a hint of annoyance when I hold up a "cute" outfit that's caught my eye in the department store next to the Bunny display. She holds up an alternate selection. A major babe outfit miniaturized.

"Over my dead body," I say, walking away. Suddenly, I feel very old. This is not going to be a happy day in Mallsville. Prozac, please.

"Do you like *Bewitched*?" she asks two weeks later. We are zipping along the twisty backroads of southern Tennessee toward home. I glance over at her. She smiles. Lip gloss sparkles in the sunlight that filters through the distant hills. Should I have put my foot down about that, I wonder.

She's going to be a heartstopper. And my heart will be the first casualty...

"I love *Bewitched*. Samantha. Serena. Endora...Who's your favorite character?" I'm assuming Nova watches *Bewitched* on Nick at Nite. Oldies for kiddies.

"I know the *Bewitched* you're talking about—that T.V. show from the black and white days. That's not the *Bewitched* I'm talking about." She furrows her brow. Indignation. Again.

"B*witched* is a group—an all-girl group from Ireland." She is trying to be patient with me. Respecting the elderly. A relic from the 'black and white' days.

C'est La Vie is her favorite *B*Witched* song. Two of the singers are twins. And one of their best songs, *To You I Belong*, was written as a tribute to their parents.

So begins my formal instruction into the murky, incongruous world of pre-adolescence. She is opening the door to her rock band and rag doll world. I must tread carefully upon her whims and wishes. Her world, constantly shifting and settling in new and unfamiliar venues, is fragile.

We pull into the driveway. Nova quickly grabs her ballet shoes from the back seat and races to greet her five cats. She loves animals. Ballet class. Being homeschooled. Living in the country. Climbing magnolia trees. And long snuggles at bedtime...she is still more little girl than rookie grown-up. But clearly straddling two worlds. 'Tween times.

Suddenly, I hear the phone ringing in the distance. I race up the steps and grab it. A voice at the other end informs me that my mother has just been placed in a nursing home. It has been just 48 hours since I put her on a plane back to Moline. How did this happen?

Listening to the details of the emergency placement, I watch through the patio door as Nova climbs a wood pile next to the nearby barn. A red-tailed hawk circles high above her. My baby. My parent. Both are leaving me. So begins the long goodbye...

—June 11, 1999 *The Dispatch*

Loss: The One Constant

(Part Four of Five Part Series)

Five hours and the phone is still ringing. A nurse, social worker, home health aide, and various concerned friends have called. Along with a half dozen unrelated business calls. Simultaneously. Who was the genius who invented call waiting??

My head is spinning. Scattered across my office desk are color-coded files labeled "Medical," "Social Services," and "Real Estate." My mother has been reduced to three files. Two more than I've allocated for either my fiancé (for whom I book business trips and speaking engagements) or my daughter (whom I homeschool). Their files have been relegated to the periphery. Of both my desk and consciousness.

Will I authorize medical treatment for my mother, inquires the director of nursing at the nursing home where my mother has been temporarily placed. She needs telephone approval for my mother to receive a physical so she can be formally admitted.

If I say yes, she gets care. And puts her absolute only asset, the house I grew up in, at risk of becoming property of the State of Illinois. If I say no, she gets turned away, but we save the house.

I take a deep breath.

Unlike the majority of my peers who have benefitted from their parent's financial generosity through the years, I supported my mother—when I could. Our tacit agreement was that she'd leave me the house in compensation.

Old news, I tell myself as I authorize the nursing home to provide whatever care necessary.

In the blink of an eye, the only home I've ever known is gone. Or soon will be.

I always knew the dreaded phone call would come. And now it had. At the worst possible time. Naturally.

Like a pesky mother-in-law, tragedy always arrives when you're at your level worst. Supremely disaffected. And chronically over-burdened. It's a fundamental law of the universe.

The deluge of phone calls is followed by something worse: silence. Time to absorb the shock. The calm before the storm.

"We are going to Moline," I announce the following day. "Grandma is sick."

Nova takes the news well. She always does. She's resilient. I am not. I am tired. Of bad news. And life in general.

The 700-mile-trip to Moline is uneventful, but tiring. If ever there is a sign of aging, it's on the road.

Once an easy day trip, the road from southern Tennessee to northern Illinois now stretches into an exhausting two-day pilgrimage.

The weather is perfect. It's been a dozen springs since I've seen Moline in May. A pity. It really is pretty. Sans winter, it wouldn't be a bad place to live. The people are the best. And the food is even better than best, I tell Nova as we head to Whitey's Ice Cream after a nutritious meal at Happy Joe's Pizza Parlor. Nothing like drowning one's sorrows in a large Turtle shake.

The weeks pass quickly. Taking care of an elderly parent and small child is a full-time unpaid job. As I'm soon reminded when my credit card is rejected. Buying St. John's Wort, of all things. The poor man's Prozac. Now rock bottom and Walgreen's will always be inextricably bound.

The paperwork—and bills—continue to mount. A daunting task. Even for a former social worker. So I've come to rely on the kindness of strangers. Like the realtor who gave me free advice about how to sell mom's house, referred me to a reasonably priced attorney and even finagled a free market analysis from a colleague. The mail carrier who brought mom's mail to the door everyday and then checked on her. The Eucharistic ministers from church who brought mom communion and prayed with her. Their kindness was trademark Moline. And so much appreciated.

Now it's time to return south to what passes for home. And wait patiently for the next chapter to unfold. Which it soon does…

"We've sold your mom's house." The realtor wanted me to be the first to know. Less than three weeks have passed since I left Moline.

The closing date is July 20, he tells me. I smile at the perfect symmetry. The anniversary of my father's untimely death 25 years ago. The beginning of many losses. First my parent. Many more over the years. And now the only home I've known.

Maybe the gods of mayhem and misery are finally satisfied. But something tells me they're not quite done with me yet...

—June 18, 1999 The Dispatch

IF THESE WALLS COULD CRY, THEY'D WEEP FOR WHAT NEVER WAS

(Part Five of Five Part Series)

I am supposed to be getting married this month. Instead, I am moving my elderly mother from Moline to Tennessee.

Repeat after me, Shalynn, life is not fair. Then try to breathe…

It wasn't going to be anything elaborate. Just a small church ceremony. A white—okay—ivory dress. Rings. The same last name. And a second chance.

Reality check. Life gets complicated when you get past eighteen, as the old song goes. And it comes with considerably more baggage: financial setbacks. Cancer. A big age gap. Elderly parents. Blending a family. The pressures of celebrity (albeit small scale).

We faced a lot of obstacles. And we even beat a few. But for every one roadblock we removed, three new ones would appear. A perpetual game of jack-in-the-box from hell. And now this…

He took the news well. After the year we've had, it's almost anti-climactic. Reality, relentless predator that it is, has intruded once again.

There is no time to mourn what won't be. Already, it is time for me to return one final time to Moline. Time to pack up mom's meager belongings. Turn over the keys for the house to its new owner. And say goodbye to the past. As if. Faulkner once said the past is never dead. Hell, it's not even in the past. He knew…

If these walls could cry, I imagine they would weep most for the family that never was. Although once, many years ago, six of us did live here together.

My grandmother and mother bought this house in the late 1940's. Without any help from a man. Or the promise that one would appear. They were independent. Ahead of their time.

Later, my dad and uncle showed up. Then my brother. And finally, me.

They're all dead now. Have been for a long time. That's what I'll always remember about this house: untimely death. No Hallmark moments. No Kodak memories. Just a lot of funerals. And empty spaces. Mostly in my heart.

As a small child, I sat at this very kitchen table, wrote my first stories and then proudly read them aloud to my mother. As a teenager, my dad and I sat across from each other at this table and discussed astronomy. We built our first telescope in the basement of this house. I first saw the rings of Saturn from this backyard.

And then there's the living room...the stories it could tell. The romances it has seen...the goodbyes it has witnessed.

My bedroom, although unimaginably small by today's standards, seemed large to me all the years I lived here. And it was the last place I got a full night of uninterrupted sleep. Twelve years ago.

As we walk outside, the realtor succinctly describes my tiny house-of-origin: 660 square feet, no amenities.

I smile silently. No amenities. But plenty of acrimony.

All in the past, I tell myself. Now it's time to move down the road.

Goodbye house. May your next owner find more peace and less tragedy than any of us did.

And now, to Tennessee with my mother. But not before I say a few farewells.

Although most of my dearest friends left the area long ago, one remains. And to that special someone who I met—and loved so long ago—thank you for always watching over me from a distance. Not only are you one of Moline's finest, you are my finest and truest friend.

To the surviving neighbors of the 'hood, thanks for helping me grow up to be the woman I that am today. Not so long ago, it didn't take a village, just a decent neighborhood to help a child get on her feet.

Special thanks also to the bus drivers, teachers, and counselors who made sure I showed up at school every day. If every troubled child had a Fred Koontz or Margie Angelo or Father Mirabelli in their lives, there would be no Columbine tragedies. Only grateful adults. Some of whom grow up to be columnists.

Finally, thanks especially to you, the readers, who have generously taken my words into your hearts and homes. Agreeing with my views or not, you allowed me to entertain and inform (hopefully) you for nearly four years. It's been a good run.

So wish me luck—and don't cry for me. Like Frosty the Snowman, I'll be back again someday. Probably in hardback.

In the meantime, thumpety, thump. Look at her go...over the hills of the South...

—June 25, 1999 *The Dispatch*

IT TAKES A VILLAGE…
AND A PRINCE TO RETURN HOME

(Part One of Two Part Series)

Twenty months ago, thanks to guilt and peer pressure, my elderly mother arrived in the foreign country of Tennessee to begin her new life as an immigrant: culturally displaced, challenged by a language barrier, uprooted from a lifetime routine, and chronically homesick.

Several columns bemoaned the plight of a lone middle-aged daughter (yours truly) struggling to provide long distance care and compassion (generating plenty of reader response, e.g., "be a good daughter and let your mother come and live with you") to a fiercely independent (read: stubborn) parent. And now…the outcome of the geriatric parent trap.

In short, she hates it here. Always has. My mother wants to go home (for once, we have something in common) desperately. She longs to see her house on 32nd Street once more. She misses her life-long friends, former employer, and favorite stores. She yearns for the familiarity and friendliness of her hometown. Moline, *aka* paradise lost. The moments and the memories of her long, but very difficult life are there, not here.

I procrastinate. I don't think she can physically make the trip. My long-distance spouse argues that psychologically, my mother must make this trip. Heart over head. Always.

We'll go to Moline Mother's Day weekend, I finally tell my mother one bright April morning as she's complaining about the heat (well, mom we do live in the South, meaning we have essentially two seasons: summer and not summer) and humidity. She is temporarily appeased. And anxious for May to arrive.

Frankly, I'm dreading the trip. And anticipating the worst. What if she falls? What if the hotel is not handicap accessible (different disabilities require different modifications and businesses usually meet only minimum guidelines)? What if she becomes inconsolably depressed upon seeing her former home and the town she left? What if…I just can't handle it? Disturbing questions.

And they are still unresolved as the plane lands in Moline the day before Mother's Day. But the gods of mayhem and misery are not far behind…within twenty-four hours, all my questions will be answered. In the worst possible way.

First, the hotel room. "These rooms are not completely accessible yet," apologizes Carl, the hotel's guest liaison. It takes a lot of time and money to retrofit hotel rooms with the necessary equipment (e.g. bathroom grab bars, elevated toilet seats, extra-wide doors). Worse, it's virtually impossible to make every handicap room totally accessible. For example, a guest who is paralyzed on the right side needs grab bars accessible from the left whereas a paraplegic needs more straight-on upper body accommodations. And so it goes.

My mother's needs are pretty comprehensive. As a seventysomething post-polio, she has both limited limb mobility and increased stiffness from the aging process.

Although the hotel is not particularly user-friendly for people such as my mother, the staff bends over backwards (nearly literally) to help us. Don, Collette, Justin, Mark, and Connie become my new best friends. To lift and transport a handicapped person, it does take a village.

However, even the supreme kindness of strangers will not prevent my mother from falling not once, but twice the second day of our trip.

Mother's Day begins as most of my days do. In crisis. First, my mother falls upon getting out of bed. Wedged between her wheelchair and the bed, she spends at least ten agonizing minutes with her immobile legs twisted like pretzels beneath her. Dead weight that I cannot move. But help finally arrives and the crisis is quelled. For five minutes.

The next fall comes in the bathroom. Same scenario. This time, the bellhop summons paramedics. Something about liability issues.

Once again, she is extricated from her predicament. But this time, her knee is badly bruised and painfully swollen. And she can't bear any weight on it. Great.

Two falls. The hotel is not accessible. And after a mind-numbing forty-five minute telephone battle with the airline that brought us here (but is incapable of getting us out of here), I must resign myself to my fate. We're stranded.

Worse, since slipping out of the hotel room late last night to visit our former home (the one I spent an entire column mourning just two months ago) in solitude—alone with my tears and memories—I, not my mother, am now inconsolably depressed. And it's not even lunchtime yet.

Suddenly, my daughter, Nova appears with a newspaper in hand. "Mom, are you single again?" she asks referring to the headline of my Mother's Day column.

"No, Mommy's still married...in theory," I tell my pint-size assistant. Somewhere out there in the New Mexico desert lives my quasi-invisible spouse.

Pointing to a nearby vending machine, I hand Nova some quarters, "Now, go get mommy some chocolate. I have a splitting headache." And clearly, a death wish.

Where's a prince when a demoralized Cinderella really needs one?

To Be Continued...

—June 26, 2001 The Dispatch

It Takes A Village...
And A Prince To Return Home

(Part Two of Two Part Series)

He arrived at the hotel bearing a sausage pizza and the patience of Job. A quiet, but decidedly reassuring manner. The ability to make and keep promises. And the kindest eyes I've seen in a long time.

He knew just what to say, how to say it, and when to say it. Even better he knew exactly when not to say anything. Instant calming effect. The best friend I've met in a long time. A fan turned friend turned platonic prince. Brad Harvey is a rarity in a world of hidden agendas and great expectations. And the major reason I survived my most recent "parental crisis" in Moline.

Our unusual friendship began with Brad writing me a fan letter four years ago. At exactly the same time I was launching my campaign to win the heart of a New Mexico writer with whom I was quite smitten. So, although I answer every reader who writes me, I was a bit distracted at the time. However, had I taken note of the shared history, common goals, and similar values espoused by my fan, my "campaign" might have been redirected toward a Moline writer. But fate had a much different plan.

Fast forward to New Years Day, 2001. An e-mail from Brad (the first in over three years) notifies me of the untimely and tragic death of our mutual friend, Chuck Trapkus. And with that single and heartbreakingly sad e-mail, a prolific correspondence begins that eventually spans hundreds of hard copy pages and brings with it the unexpected gift of a sane friend just when I most need one.

Death and new beginnings. A fascinating juxtaposition of events. Serendipity. Vintage Shalynn stuff.

Through the months, we've exchanged high school horror stories (Brad's a Maroon, I'm a Pioneer, and we're both survivors of the Class of '76), commiserated with each other about the many romantic disasters that have punctured our respective hearts through the years, and generically "vented" constantly about life's little injustices, namely, that Pulitzer Prize that eludes us. Two disgruntled freelance writers and a large vocabulary are a dangerous combination.

Recently, we even took the ultimate leap of faith and decided to collaborate long distance on a variety of creative projects including a screenplay (next stop, Hollywood). Twice the talent, half the problems (sorry, shameless self-promotion rearing its ugly head), we figure.

But until this trip to Moline, Brad and I had never met in person. And now, here he stood, appearing like an angel of mercy in the midst of my latest crisis. Bearing gifts of food and friendship. Somebody to watch over me, as the song goes.

Each day Brad appeared at the hotel, with no agenda other than helping me to help my elderly mother stay in Moline for four days to visit the friends and familiar spots she misses so deeply. To help me make this huge dream come true for my mother in spite of even larger obstacles. Including the aftermath of two falls within one day.

He physically lifted my mother into bed at night, helped her in and out of her wheelchair during the day (as a bonus blessing, Brad worked with the elderly at a local adult daycare for nearly eight years, so he knew the proper body mechanics—and psychology to use), fed us yummy pizza and ice cream, brought his daughters, Nikki, Kristin, and Josie to entertain my daughter, Nova, and provided transportation around town on short notice.

More importantly, Brad symbolically held my hand through one of the most difficult times of my recent life.

It's not everybody who can sit quietly with me while I brood about my mother's failing health and obsess endlessly about a multitude of professional, marital, and financial problems. Brad can. And does. Graciously and with endless patience.

No unsolicited advice or express lane solutions. Just quiet reassurance. Pandering to my neurotic needs with a magical smile and megadoses of chocolate. A real pal that gets the emotional drift. A keeper. Especially since kindred spirits are so hard to come by.

The days pass without further incident. However, my mother's knee remains swollen and badly bruised. But she doesn't complain.

She is, after all, exactly where she wants to be. Home. At last. And, probably for the last time.

That's what made it imperative that we stay as long as we could. And thanks to my dear friend Brad (and the many others who helped me make this dream of my mother's come true), this is one story with a reasonably happy ending.

Upon returning to Tennessee, my mother was hospitalized immediately, and as I write this, is recovering at a convalescent center. My long-distance spouse is on his way here. There are screenplays to finish and lives to be lived. Even a dream or two still waiting to be realized.

And the journey continues…

—July 5, 2001 *The Dispatch*

* * *

Author's Note: A few months after this article was originally published, my "long-distance spouse" and I divorced. Brad and I later married, but divorced in 2009. Regardless of our differences, Brad remained a devoted "son" to my mother, who died on April 15, 2012.

AFTERWORD

—November 2012

One day, at the age of thirty-seven, I had an epiphany—out of my previous forty-three jobs (I started working for pay as a housekeeper, at the age of ten, so I had a long work history), there had not been one I had even remotely enjoyed. Admittedly, some were less miserable than others, but none had ever sparked any real passion.

What I really wanted to do was pure folly. Unspeakably reckless and irresponsible. Deep down, you see, I wanted to be a writer. A wordsmith. A woman of letters. As I said, utter foolishness.

Deciding on the threshold of turning forty to become a writer is kind of like deciding to become an actor or politician. Or both. Defined by delusion and rock bottom on the career respectability index, but with far more obscurity and far less financial security. At least politicians can take bribes to generate secondary incomes and actors have day jobs to fall back or forward on.

"Thirty days to the homeless shelter," predicted my stunned colleagues at the university where I was teaching on the eve of my epiphany. "What are you thinking?"

Call it a midlife crisis, but in spite of all the dire predictions about would happen to me if I became a full-time writer (read: failure and poverty on a grand scale), I knew I had to do something dramatically different with the rest of my life. Fast. I was staring down the wrong end of forty and seeing nothing ahead but a dreary and dismal midlife followed by certain death (now in my mid-fifties, I acknowledge the absurdity of my thirtysomething thinking, but then hindsight, without the cataracts of youth, is perfect vision).

Armed with an incredible sense of urgency, the determination of a dictator, and the basic inability to take "no" for an answer, I set out to find an enlightened editor willing to take a chance on an unknown writer. Against all odds, I found several in various states. Five editors in particular had a profound impact on my work: Kenda Burrows and Joe Payne at The *Moline (IL) Dispatch*, John Ehinger at The *Huntsville (AL) Times*, the late Bob Kyer at The *Tul-*

lahoma (TN) News, and Anthony Spence at *The Tennessee Register*. Each took the time to encourage and support an emerging writer, who with no formal training or background in journalism, plunged in, heart to the page. Each published my work regularly for over a dozen years, even as the newspaper business itself was dying, and their own jobs were in jeopardy. Each represents the best of print journalism. And to each, I am truly grateful.

Ice On The Wing began as a collection of columns about the personal, political, and parenting experiences of a thirty—and then—forty-something writer who experienced the world in fifty shades of black. Except when it came to my daughter, Nova, who reminded me that every now and then, the angels do prevail. As this project expanded and eventually took on a life of its own, *Ice On The Wing* became more an emotional lifeline than a collection of words from long ago.

Now in my fifties(read: somewhere between irrelevant and dead) and facing many uncertainties does not inspire a lot of optimism. So you dodge the ice today—another glacier awaits tomorrow. We're just rearranging deck chairs at this point, awaiting the inevitable collision with death. At least that's how it often feels.

There is, no doubt, a certain irreverent cynicism born of chronic loss at work in my world view. Beginning with my multiple marriages and subsequent divorces. I now understand why I did not do well in Father Eck's Marriage and Family class. I told the radical priest up front that taking the required course on marriage was a waste of my time because I had no intention of ever getting married. I then proceeded to sit silently and sulk, tuning out everything he said. It was 1976, I was a senior at the local Catholic high school, and I knew myself better than anyone. Most of all, I knew instinctively that I should avoid marriage. If I'd only listened to my 17-year-old self and joined the convent…

Instead, I married. Divorced. Remarried. Divorced. Remarried. Divorced again. And, I'm almost embarrassed to admit—remarried yet again. For those keeping score, that's four ice storms, three wings sheared off mid-flight. I don't get it myself. I am the least optimistic person I know, and yet, I keep thinking every time I'll get it right. Until I don't. But maybe this time, I did. Or else we're both just too old to care.

In any case, my one and only true husband (based on the fact that we have been best friends for nearly a decade, have seen each other at our level worst, and still tolerate each other), Steven Womack, has been an integral part of bringing *Ice On The Wing* to fruition. After my mother's tragic death earlier this year, I felt totally lost and overwhelmed by grief. I desperately needed something to give me a sense of direction and meaning. I needed to retreat to my sanctuary: writing.

I went to Steve, an award-winning author and editor, and asked him to set aside his own work to help me resurrect my comatose writing career, basically to give me a reason to live. And without complaint or even question, he quietly set himself to the tedious task of copyediting and typesetting the hodge-podge of articles and columns that would in time become *Ice On The Wing*. For his guidance and eternal patience, I am beyond grateful.

Sadly, many of the people who graced the pages of *Ice On The Wing* have died since their stories were originally published. Including my mother, Roseann Gillespie, who passed away just seven months ago, at the age of ninety. Together, we endured eleven hospitalizations, each ending with the same words of hopelessness, six nursing home placements, and countless hours of solitary waiting for her suffering to end. She died in slow motion as my daughter grew from a child into an adult. And as a result, all three of us died in different ways.

My forthcoming memoir, *Life In The House of Death*, is the story of our tortured journey with my mother as she entered the final stages of her life. One painful step at a time.

While my mother's story predictably ended in death, my daughter Nova is just beginning her life. Now 22, Nova and I completed our remarkable homeschool journey in 2008 when she graduated, with Honors, from our regional Home Education Program. One of eighty-three homeschool graduates, Nova was named Outstanding Senior in the Class of 2008 and received a full-ride Presidential Scholarship to attend Middle Tennessee State University. Four years later, on May 5, 2012, Nova graduated *summa cum laude* with a Bachelor's degree in—wait for it—English and Spanish. The student has now surpassed her teacher in two languages!

After graduation, Nova and I started *Creative Capers*, a writing-editing-proofreading service. Between Nova's astute artistic and editorial eye (she designed the cover for **Ice On The Wing** and then spent countless hours typing and copyediting the manuscript) and my unflinching sense of the human condition as well as our endless supply of ink and ideas, we make a great team. Twice the talent and half the trouble. Just like our homeschool days.

And the stories we'll have…